BUDDHISM
WHAT EVERYONE NEEDS TO KNOW®

BUDDHISM

WHAT EVERYONE NEEDS TO KNOW®

DALE S. WRIGHT

OXFORD
UNIVERSITY PRESS

Oxford University Press is a department of the University of Oxford. It furthers
the University's objective of excellence in research, scholarship, and education
by publishing worldwide. Oxford is a registered trade mark of Oxford University
Press in the UK and certain other countries.

"What Everyone Needs to Know" is a registered trademark of
Oxford University Press

Published in the United States of America by Oxford University Press
198 Madison Avenue, New York, NY 10016, United States of America.

© Oxford University Press 2020

Library of Congress Cataloging-in-Publication Data
Names: Wright, Dale S, author.
Title: Buddhism : what everyone needs to know / Dale S. Wright.
Description: New York, NY : Oxford University Press, [2020] |
Includes bibliographical references and index.
Identifiers: LCCN 2019021020 | ISBN 9780190843670 (hardback) |
ISBN 9780190843663 (paperback) | ISBN 9780190843687 (updf) |
ISBN 9780190843694 (epub)
Subjects: LCSH: Buddhism.
Classification: LCC BQ4022 .W75 2020 | DDC 294.3—dc23
LC record available at https://lccn.loc.gov/2019021020

1 3 5 7 9 8 6 4 2

Paperback printed by LSC Communications, United States of America
Hardback printed by Bridgeport National Bindery, Inc., United States of America

CONTENTS

Introduction   1

1. Origins and Early History   6

1.1. *When and where did Buddhism begin?*   6

1.2. *What was the religious and cultural setting in which Buddhism was born?*   7

1.3. *Who was the Buddha?*   8

1.4.   *To what extent is this traditional story about the life of the Buddha historically accurate?*   11

1.5. *What do the various names and titles of the Buddha mean, and how do they reflect the early Buddhists' understanding of the Buddha?*   12

1.6.   *What kind of life did the Buddha live, and why did he call it the Middle Path?*   14

1.7.   *Who were the early disciples of the Buddha, and what kinds of lives did they live?*   16

1.8.   *How did early Buddhists conceive of themselves as a community, or sangha?*   17

1.9.   *What was the role of women in the early Buddhist community?*   19

1.10.   *What were the rules that governed the lives of monks and nuns?*   20

1.11. What was the relationship between members of the monastic community and lay Buddhists?   23

1.12. What kinds of religious involvement were available to the lay community?   24

1.13. How did early Buddhists align themselves with the northern Indian social system, especially the early stages of the Indian caste system?   25

1.14. What are the sacred texts of Buddhism?   26

1.15. What issues do the early Buddhist sutras address, and how were these texts used in practice?   28

1.16. What was the relationship between Buddhism and other Indian religious traditions in this early period?   29

1.17. When and how did the Buddha die?   30

1.18. What happened to the Buddhist community following the death of the Buddha?   32

2. Buddhist Diversity   35

2.1. How and when did Buddhism spread beyond its origins in northeastern India?   35

2.2. What are the primary sectarian divisions within Buddhism, and how did they develop?   36

2.3. What are the distinguishing characteristics of Buddhism in the Southeast Asian cultures of Myanmar, Thailand, Laos, and Cambodia, and how are these Buddhist cultures linked to Buddhist traditions in Sri Lanka?   39

2.4. What are Mahayana sutras, and how are they different from earlier texts associated with the Buddha?   40

2.5. How many sutras are there, and to what extent do Buddhists read them?   42

2.6. Among these many Buddhist sutras, which ones are most important to read to get a good sense of Buddhist sacred texts?   43

2.7. Besides the sutras, are there other Buddhist texts that have been equally influential in the development of Buddhism? 45

2.8. Why and how is the Silk Road significant in Buddhist history?   46

2.9. How was Buddhism introduced and assimilated into an already established and sophisticated Chinese culture?   48

2.10. What are the most distinctive features of Buddhism in China, Vietnam, Korea, and Japan?   51

2.11. How did Buddhism take hold in Tibet and Mongolia, and how did these cultures develop their own unique Buddhist style?   54

2.12. What is Tantric Buddhism, and how has it developed as a unique form of Buddhism?   58

2.13. What is Zen Buddhism?   59

2.14. Why did Buddhism disappear from India after being disseminated virtually everywhere else in Asia?   63

2.15. How has Buddhism been shaped by contact with the West?   64

2.16. How did Western Buddhism emerge, and how is it related to Asian Buddhism?   67

3. Buddhist Teachings   71

3.1. Do Buddhists believe in God?   71

3.2. What are the Four Noble Truths?   72

3.3. Does the emphasis on human suffering make Buddhism pessimistic?   75

3.4. What other teachings about the causes of suffering are important in Buddhism?   76

3.5. What are the delusions that Buddhists regard as detrimental to life?   76

3.6. How do Buddhists understand the impermanence of all things?   78

3.7. What does dependent arising mean, and what role does it play in Buddhist thought and practice?   79

3.8. What does the Buddhist teaching of no-soul or no-self mean?   81

3.9. If there is no self or no soul, what then am I? How do Buddhists understand being a person?   83

3.10. How do Buddhists understand death and the possibility of an afterlife?   85

3.11. What is the Buddhist understanding of karma?   86

3.12.   How is karma related to the Buddhist idea of rebirth or
        reincarnation, and how is this afterlife thought to work?   88

3.13.   What role do karma and rebirth play in Buddhist moral culture?   91

3.14.   What is the Buddhist view of the larger cosmos?   93

3.15.   Does faith play a role in Buddhism? And if so, what?   95

3.16.   What further teachings distinguish Mahayana Buddhism
        from earlier traditions of Buddhism?   96

3.17.   What is the Mahayana bodhisattva ideal, and how does it
        differ from the image of the Buddhist saint in earlier Theravada
        Buddhist traditions?   98

3.18.   What is the Mahayana Buddhist teaching of emptiness, and
        how it is related to the bodhisattva's quest for wisdom and
        compassion?   100

3.19.   How did the Buddhist understanding of the Buddha evolve?   102

3.20.   What elements of teaching are distinct to the Tantric tradition? 105

3.21.   What are the basic teachings of devotional Buddhism?   107

3.22.   What are the primary teachings of Zen Buddhism, and what
        role do they play in Zen practice?   109

3.23.   What are the primary rules, virtues, and vices in Buddhist
        morality?   113

3.24.   What is Buddhist enlightenment? Is that what nirvana means?   116

4. Buddhist Practices   **120**

4.1.   What is the relationship between Buddhist teachings and
        the practice of Buddhism?   120

4.2.   How is Buddhist practice related to karma and the goal of
        enlightenment?   121

4.3.   What aspects of life are thought to be affected by Buddhist
        practice?   123

4.4.   What is Buddhist meditation?   125

4.5.   What are the primary forms or styles of Buddhist meditation?   126

4.6.   What do Buddhist practitioners do in meditation?   130

4.7.   Why is bodily posture considered important in the practice
        of meditation?   134

4.8. Is prayer an important practice in Buddhism? 136

4.9. What practices of moral self-cultivation play a significant
role in Buddhism? 137

4.10. Are there recognizable stages along the path of
Buddhist practice? 139

4.11. Are there ascetic practices that are important for
Buddhists? 142

4.12. What role does ritual play in Buddhist practice? 144

4.13. How do scripture and reading function in Buddhist practice? 147

4.14. Are artistic images of the Buddha important in settings of
Buddhist practice? 149

4.15. Do sacred sites and pilgrimages have a function in Buddhist
practice? 150

4.16. Is art or music employed in Buddhist practice? 152

4.17. What role do priests, gurus, or other religious professionals
play for Buddhist practitioners? 154

4.18. How is Tantric practice distinct from earlier forms of Buddhist
practice? 156

4.19. How has Zen practice developed in its own distinct way? 159

4.20. Do Buddhists try to win converts? 162

5. Contemporary Global Buddhism 165

5.1. Is Buddhism a religion, and if so in what sense? 165

5.2. Why is Buddhism currently of interest around the world? 168

5.3. How does Buddhism compare to other major world religions
in terms of its age and number of participants? 170

5.4. How does Buddhism relate to government and politics? 171

5.5. What is the relationship between Buddhism and modern
science, and why is this connection so frequently
emphasized today? 173

5.6. Isn't there a conflict between basic Buddhist values and the
character of modern capitalism? 175

5.7. What is the relationship between Buddhism and modern
psychology? 178

5.8. What is secular Buddhism, and how has Buddhism adjusted to
      the overall secular character of contemporary global society?   181

5.9. Who is the Dalai Lama?   184

5.10. Who are the other most widely known or important
      Buddhist leaders?   186

5.11. What positions have Buddhist leaders taken on issues of
      violence, war, and peace?   189

5.12. What can we learn from Buddhism about nature and the
      environment? What are ecoBuddhism and Green Buddhism?   191

5.13. After having virtually disappeared from its country of origin,
      has Buddhism been revived in modern India?   194

5.14. How have Buddhists responded to the easing of restrictions
      on religion in China?   196

5.15. How have Buddhist humanitarian organizations and women's
      leadership in them begun to transform East Asian Buddhism?   199

5.16. What is the status of Buddhism in Tibet? What about Tibetan
      Buddhism in exile?   201

5.17. How does Buddhism deal with controversial issues like
      divorce, abortion, and suicide?   203

5.18. What holidays and festivals are celebrated by modern
      Buddhists, and are there modern pilgrimages that Buddhists
      consider important?   206

5.19. How have the roles of women in Buddhism changed in
      contemporary cultures, both in Asia and in the temples
      and meditation centers of Western Buddhism?   209

5.20. How is the contemporary practice of mindfulness in secular
      settings such as schools and hospitals related to Buddhist
      traditions of meditation?   211

5.21. What are the future prospects for Buddhism?   214

SUGGESTIONS FOR FURTHER READING   215
INDEX   219

INTRODUCTION

Why would everyone need to know anything about Buddhism? One important reason is that no matter who you are or where you live, Buddhism is part of your cultural environment. Whether we know it or not, most of us have Buddhist neighbors or communities of Buddhists living not far away. Now more than ever mutual understanding between people from different cultural backgrounds is crucial. We live and work together. We share the same trains, schools, shopping centers, theaters, and everything else, and mutual understanding is the key to productive, peaceful coexistence.

But getting along with others isn't the only reason to introduce yourself to Buddhism, nor even the best one. There is much that all of us can learn from each other, knowledge that may in fact prove to be quite useful in shaping our own ways of living. Many of us have been doing that for decades—taking an interest in cultural, religious, and philosophical traditions different from our own as a way to stretch our minds, to broaden our understanding not just of other people but of the many admirable ways to think about the world and the many ways to live creatively and responsibly within it.

In this respect many people who were not raised Buddhists have discovered that Buddhism has a lot to offer. Among the world's religions it is certainly unique. Indeed, even though

Westerners have been interested in Buddhism for almost two centuries, debate still continues over what Buddhism is. Is it a religion? A philosophy? A way of life? A set of techniques for mental and psychological enhancement? It appears to function in all of these ways and continues to impress observers with the range of values it offers.

One way that Buddhism is currently influencing contemporary global culture is through the practice of mindfulness. Mindfulness training—cultivated as an offshoot of centuries of sophisticated Buddhist meditation practices—is to be found virtually everywhere around us. It is being taught in schools as an effective means of building the capacity for concentration, learning, and creativity. Hospitals are teaching mindfulness exercises as proven methods of stress reduction, as techniques for radical pain relief, and much more. Mindfulness is being taught in police departments, in the advanced technology labs of Silicon Valley, in churches, movie studios, research institutions, and the military. Instruction in mindfulness is now provided to professional athletes, surgeons, senior citizens, and in almost any setting we can imagine. Although we don't necessarily need to understand the Buddhist origins of mindfulness to benefit from it, having that knowledge certainly does put us in a position to appropriate it in more thoughtful and innovative ways.

But mindfulness is just one aspect of Buddhism. For a functional and well-rounded understanding of Buddhism much more is required. Knowing about the Buddha himself and about the origins of Buddhism is a good place to start. It is also important to understand how Buddhism spread throughout Asia, how it diversified into a number of different sects and styles, and how these have evolved over the many centuries of Buddhist history. You would certainly want to know the basic teachings of Buddhism and the various practices in which Buddhists engage, with perhaps special attention to Buddhist meditation since that has become so widely practiced all over the world. Well-informed readers might also want to ask questions about contemporary global Buddhism, such as the position of Buddhism in the world today.

This book is my best effort to provide that background, to offer a well-rounded account of Buddhism for intelligent readers from many different backgrounds. Although I certainly can't claim to know everything about Buddhism, I have been fascinated by it for much of my life, studying as many dimensions of this tradition as possible while writing books and essays about particular aspects of it. I've been teaching college students the basics of Buddhism for almost four decades, mostly at Occidental College in Los Angeles, where I have spent much of my career, but occasionally by invitation from Asian and other Western universities. In other words, there is a sense in which I've been writing this book for most of my life without ever knowing it. So when Oxford University Press invited me to author a book in this series, I knew the time had come to accept the challenge to compose a cogent, user-friendly introduction to Buddhism.

Before beginning, you may want to ask whether I am a Buddhist. The honest answer is I'm not sure. But this much is clear: If you study something that interests you with an open mind for a very long time it will surely seep into you. You will be affected by it. It will change who you are at least to some degree. In fact, from the very outset that was my hope, even a commitment that I made to myself. I would seek to learn both *about* Buddhism and *from* it. While learning everything I could about what Buddhism was and is, I would allow it to influence my own way of life whenever that seemed desirable or wise. That's the point of the great wisdom traditions of the world. There is much to learn from them to the benefit of us all.

Given this commitment, when I study Buddhism I ask myself what of value I can learn from it. And when Buddhists explained that their way of thinking on these important human matters can be fully understood only in tandem with the practice of meditation, I took their word for it and engaged in this practice. I visit Buddhist people and Buddhist temples all over the world whenever I can and ask myself what can be learned from them. I suspect that sounds very Buddhist. But I've never been initiated or officially accepted as a Buddhist. No individual serves as my guru or teacher, and no particular sect of Buddhism recognizes me as one of their own. I'm not a monk nor a temple member, nor have I taken vows or anything of an official Buddhist nature. So, am I a Buddhist? I still don't know. But for the purposes of this book I'm perfectly willing to let you decide.

Two points before we begin. One is that, like other books in this series, this book is organized from beginning to end in question-and-answer format. This inquiry-based structure fits the topic very well. A number of Buddhist scriptures were composed in dialogue style, disciples posing questions to the Buddha and the Buddha teaching by putting questions directly back to them in order to encourage their own independent reflection. Still, this aspect of the book may seem somewhat one-sided. I do both the asking and the answering! In each case, however, these questions are derived from those that students have been asking me for years. Very often their curiosity has been right on target, but sometimes it takes some persuasion from me—here is what you should be asking if you want to learn what you need to know to have a functional overall understanding of Buddhism.

A second point, related to the first, is that many choices have been made to prevent the book from swelling in size to become a burden on the reader. Many topics—important Buddhist people, places, teachings, practices—are not included here. Some of these are just as interesting as what did get included. Judgment calls in these cases were inevitable and could have easily gone in other directions. This book is therefore truly an introduction, a basic overview that aims to cover just enough to provide a solid working account of the whole of Buddhism. For those who would like to probe further, suggestions for further reading are included at the end. But there are other ways to go further in understanding. There are Buddhist communities, temples, and meditation centers virtually everywhere in the world, and a visit to almost any of these would be an excellent way to take a step beyond "what everyone needs to know." But first, here's what you need to know.

1

ORIGINS AND EARLY HISTORY

1.1. When and where did Buddhism begin?

Like Christianity and Islam, the last two of the five major
world religions to emerge, Buddhism has an identifiable
founder, Siddhartha Gautama, who came to be called the
Buddha. Gautama was born in a village in the low Himalayan
foothills of northeastern India—today just across the border
into Nepal. When he came of age, however, Gautama set out
on a religious quest, traveling on foot across the broad plain
of the Ganges River in search of the most famous spiritual
teachers of the time. Six years later, upon his attainment of
enlightenment at Bodh Gaya, not far from the sacred city of
Benares (Varanasi), Gautama became the Buddha, meaning
the Enlightened One, thus initiating the long tenure of the
Buddhist tradition.

Although the traditional dates for the life of the Buddha are
566–486 BCE, or 563–483 BCE, depending on which tradition
we consult, historians today tend to agree that the Buddha's
life occupied the middle of the fifth century BCE, and his death
occurred sometime before 400 BCE. Reliable historical evidence for any theory attempting to date the life of the Buddha
is scarce, however. What is certain is that Buddhism began
in northeastern India over four centuries before the advent
of Christianity and gradually spread throughout South Asia,

Central Asia, East Asia, and Southeast Asia to become one of the most successful of all the world's religions.

1.2. What was the religious and cultural setting in which Buddhism was born?

Although Buddhism appears very early in human history, the history of Indian civilization goes back much further. By the time the Buddha was born, the cultures of South Asia had experienced well over a thousand years of documentable development. Archaeological ruins along the Indus River dating back as far as two millennia BCE give us a view of the development of numerous urban agricultural centers. But for reasons so far largely unknown, this early and mysterious Neolithic civilization appears to have declined and, beginning as early as 1500 BCE, given way to a new wave of migrating nomadic tribes that brought the Vedic cultures of the Indo-Aryans into South Asia. Arriving in waves over several centuries of migration, these warrior tribes occupied the northern Indian plains and settled in for centuries of cultural evolution. This Vedic culture of northern India was articulated in ancient Sanskrit, which is historically related to ancient Greek and Persian as well as Lithuanian and other spoken languages, and over time this became the classical language of India and of Buddhism.

Many of the distinct characteristics of Vedic culture helped shape Buddhism. Organized by separate social classes or castes—priests, warriors, farmers, and the cultural outsiders who would work for them as laborers—Vedic culture was highly formal, segregated, and ritualized. Like ancient Greek religion, Vedic religion required ritual appeasement of numerous gods and goddesses, which gave rise to a rich literary and poetic tradition. As this previously nomadic culture stabilized and reoriented itself around agriculture, and as new Iron Age technology emerged to help expand the population and the number of urban centers, new spiritual concerns emerged as well.

Just prior to the birth of Buddhism, a new set of Sanskrit religious and philosophical texts documented the rise of a new kind of spiritual quest that tended to ignore the Vedic gods altogether. The *Upanisads*, written prior to and after the emergence of Buddhism, reject worldly accomplishment and advocate a life of ascetic contemplation in the wilderness. Those who followed this new kind of religious quest sought answers to the quandaries of human existence in personal experience and began to practice a wide variety of meditation techniques. The Buddha and his early followers would have been considered just one of these new religious groups, although they were unique in rejecting some of the basic principles of the dominant Vedic culture.

1.3. Who was the Buddha?

The traditional story about the life of the Buddha, learned and admired by billions of Buddhists over many centuries, goes roughly like this: The Buddha was born a prince of the Shakya people in northeastern India. His birth took place in Lumbini, a grove outside the town of Kapilavastu. He was named Siddhartha, meaning "One who has achieved his goal." His mother, Maya, who had been impregnated miraculously in a dream, died seven days after his birth. The royal child would be raised by her sister, Prajapati, who married Gautama's father. Signs of the child's magnificence were immediately evident, and when the wise men of the area examined the young prince, they predicted that he would lead an extraordinary life, either as the greatest of all kings or as the great spiritual emancipator who would make enlightenment available to all of humanity.

These traditions tell us that although the child showed profound sensitivity to the hardships of human existence, his father would distract him from these religious concerns in order to encourage the young prince to fulfill his birthright as a great king. Surrounded by luxury and separated from the struggles of the people outside of the palace, Gautama grew up to marry, have a son, and participate fully in the privileged life of the local aristocracy. Upon coming of age, however, the prince requested the opportunity to see the kingdom over which he would rule, and his father consented to a series of chariot rides out into the real world. Desiring to further shield his son from the harsh realities endured by most of his subjects, the king ordered that all difficult and unsightly affairs be removed from the path of the chariot and that the driver not discuss these troubling matters with the prince.

On the first ride into town, however, the gods intervened. They arranged that a feeble elderly man would be visible and that the chariot driver would forget his vow and explain to the prince that this decrepit state is the fate of all human beings—even the strong and vital will grow old and weak. On the second ride Gautama saw someone who was desperately ill, and the driver explained that sickness too is the lot of all human beings. On the third ride, they saw a corpse, and the chariot driver said that everyone who is born will also die. Stunned by the suffering and impermanence of human existence, the prince ordered a fourth and final ride, on which he witnessed a religious mendicant, a wanderer intent on discovering the meaning of human life.

These realizations led to what the tradition calls "the great renunciation." Renouncing the life of worldly pleasure, Gautama abandoned his royal destiny and his family, and at the age of twenty-nine, left home in pursuit of wisdom. Without servants or money, and wearing the clothing of voluntary poverty, the former prince walked through the countryside in search of spiritual guidance and inspiration. His first teacher, Alara Kalama, taught meditation techniques through which deep mental trance could be attained. Buddhist traditions maintain that Siddhartha quickly mastered these spiritual practices and was offered equal standing as a teacher and religious leader. Although he had absorbed these meditation techniques and appreciated their effects, Siddhartha realized that they still didn't solve the deepest questions of human existence, and he departed to continue his search.

Locating another of the famous spiritual guides of his time, the young seeker became a meditation student of Uddaka Ramaputta, who taught an even more refined meditation practice through which consciousness would seemingly be transcended. When Gautama quickly mastered these techniques, Uddaka yielded to his natural superiority and asked to become his disciple. Still not satisfied with what he had learned, Gautama set out to practice the most extreme austerities and joined a group of five ascetics who sought total mastery of mind over matter, spirit over body. Limiting his consumption of oxygen and his intake of food, Gautama practiced a self-mortification so extreme that he eventually became emaciated and weak.

Temporarily resting in the shade of a tree, Gautama entered a state of deep mental calm, one that he recalled from his youth. He realized then that any serious spiritual quest would require physical stability and strength and that proper nourishment for the body was essential. A woman walking by the tree noticed his malnourished state and offered him some milk. Seeing that Gautama had yielded to the temptations of the body, the five ascetics denounced him and walked away. Remaining there under what would later be called "the Bodhi Tree," the Tree of Awakening, Gautama found himself enjoying both deep meditation and profound insight. Traditional legends claim that at this point, Mara, the tempter or Satan figure in Indian mythology, became alarmed at the prospect that a human being might achieve true enlightenment and plotted a series of events to distract Gautama. When neither divine maidens nor ferocious storms lured the seeker out of his deep concentration, Mara challenged Gautama to a contest of powers. In response, the future Buddha simply reached down and touched the ground, whereupon the entire earth attested to Gautama's achievement. As Mara fled in defeat, Gautama continued to sit in meditation, culminating that night in what Buddhists regard as full and complete enlightenment.

Gautama remained under the Bodhi Tree for several weeks to absorb the full impact of his achievement. Having attained enlightenment and become the Buddha at the age of thirty-five, he decided that his destiny would be to become a guide and teacher leading others along the path of spiritual emancipation. Traveling toward the sacred city of Benares, the Buddha approached the five ascetics who had renounced him some weeks before. Although resolved among themselves to ignore the self-indulgent Gautama, the five were immediately drawn into the enlightened aura they witnessed in the Buddha's demeanor. When the Buddha offered them their first taste of the dharma—the Buddhist teachings—all five experienced some degree of insight and immediately became the Buddha's first disciples, the first members of the sangha, the Buddhist spiritual community. This pattern of meditative practice and teaching would continue for as many as forty-five years—the Buddha and members of the sangha wandering through the countryside, practicing meditation, cultivating wisdom, and teaching when asked.

1.4. To what extent is this traditional story about the life of the Buddha historically accurate?

Numerous complications render any modern quest for the historical Buddha problematic. Siddhartha wrote nothing himself, nor did his immediate followers. The teachings of the Buddha were memorized by early disciples and then passed down orally to their disciples. When these sutras were first written down in the early centuries of Buddhism, little attention was given to describing the Buddha's life since they were primarily concerned with what he taught. Because the sutras were originally talks or sermons the Buddha had given, they do contain occasional references to his own life, but only sporadically. Stories of the Buddha's life were no doubt important in the early centuries of Buddhism, and these circulated orally from one place and time to another. Yet no attempt to gather all of these stories into a full written account of the life of the Buddha appeared until five centuries after his death. The most important of these biographies—the *Mahavastu* (Great Story), the *Lalitavistara* (Graceful Account), and the *Buddhacarita* (Acts of the Buddha)—were composed in the first and second centuries of the Common Era.

Furthermore, as we can immediately glean from their titles, the primary concern of these biographies was inspirational, not historical. The authors were not particularly concerned with the accuracy of their account and did not hesitate to include a variety of embellishments that had accrued over centuries of oral tradition and that give these stories their exceptionally fine-grained literary character. Given the scarcity of historical evidence, assessing the story in terms of its impact or influence is probably our best means of access to it. To be born and educated in a Buddhist culture is to have some version of this story imprinted on one's imagination and character and thus to evaluate one's own life in relation to this ideal. Indeed, judging just in terms of historical impact, the Buddha's life narrative would have to be considered one of the greatest, most significant stories ever told.

1.5. What do the various names and titles of the Buddha mean, and how do they reflect the early Buddhists' understanding of the Buddha?

First of all, it should be clear from the fact that we refer to "the Buddha" that this is a title rather than a name. In the same sense that "Christ" isn't Jesus's last name but rather a title— Jesus who was the Christ (the "anointed one," the savior or redeemer)—"Buddha" (derived from "bodhi," or awakening) is a title that at some point after his "awakening" or enlightenment was given to Gautama. Siddhartha was his given name at birth, meaning "One who has hit his mark" or "One who has achieved his goal." Siddhartha's family name was Gautama, which you will frequently see spelled Gotama. Putting all this together, we would say that Siddhartha Gautama became the Buddha upon his awakening under the Bodhi Tree at the age of thirty-five.

Another descriptive title that has been frequently used in reference to the Buddha is Shakyamuni. Recall that the Buddha was a member of the Shakya tribe in northern India, so that portion of this word refers to his being a member of this ethnic group. "Muni" means sage, wise man, so "Shakyamuni" identifies the Buddha as the sage of the Shakya group. Another early title—Tathagata—is a frequently used synonym for the Buddha, especially in later Mahayana Buddhism. Tathagata means "One who has thus come" and refers to the arrival of the Buddha or sometimes the arrival of one of many Buddhas into the world. Other frequently seen titles for the Buddha are "World Honored One" and "the Enlightened One"; these carry connotations that include religious devotion.

The earliest converts to Buddhism, those who encountered the Buddha while journeying on their religious quests and who decided to follow him, no doubt regarded Gautama as yet another spiritual teacher, one of several or even many they may have encountered. The fact that they decided to follow him and to become his disciple no doubt indicates that they regarded the Buddha as the most worthy of these teachers. But no matter how high their regard for their new teacher, it is extremely unlikely that any of his disciples thought of the Buddha as anything but a human being—a wise human being to be sure, even one who had fully awakened to the truth about human life, but still a human being like all others. Because beliefs about repeated lifetimes or reincarnations were already by that time quite common in India, some followers would have assumed that the Buddha, having achieved this exalted state, would have already ascended to the highest level of human incarnation. Nevertheless, they followed someone who was fully human, who suffered many of the same ailments they did, who had disagreements, who like them was power-less in the face of kings and military leaders. The Buddha lived through the turmoil of life to the age of eighty, and then, like everyone else, he died.

By the time the Buddha died, however, his reputation was widespread and exalted. He was famous as the religious leader of a new kind of spiritual practice and way of under-standing the world. His followers, who had grown in number, no doubt proclaimed his virtues as strongly as they could. As Buddhism grew, so did the Buddha's reputation. He was *the* Buddha, the one who could be said to be fully enlightened (al-though other groups no doubt made similar claims about their founders). And as Buddhism expanded into new lands, new ways to understand who or what the Buddha was emerged. We will address these issues later in the book. But for the earliest Buddhists, it should be clear that they followed an extremely impressive human being on whose life they could model their own.

1.6. What kind of life did the Buddha live, and why did he call it the Middle Path?

From the time of his awakening at about age thirty-five to the end of his life at about age eighty, the Buddha continued to wander through the northern Indian plains as he had since renouncing his royal heritage at age twenty-nine. He lived without personal possessions, without financial resources, and without a home in order to devote his life in its entirety to spiritual practices and teaching. The Buddha neither married · again nor returned to his wife and refrained from sexual ac-tivity throughout his teaching career. He traveled incessantly, slept on the ground without bedding, and sustained himself on food given to him by working people whom he encountered along his path.

The extreme difficulty of such a life is apparent to our eyes and was to the eyes of people in the Buddha's own time.

Nevertheless, he proclaimed this way of life the Middle Path between two unfruitful ways of inhabiting the earth. On one extreme is a life of sensual indulgence. Recall that this was Gautama's own upbringing. Raised in luxury and pampered by his royal father, the Buddha's renunciation indicated his rejection of a life of self-indulgence as spiritually unfulfilling. On the other extreme, however, is a life of self-mortification. This was Gautama's adopted practice for several years as a wandering ascetic. He fasted, exposed himself to discomfort and pain, and understood this austerity as a way to free his spirit and mind from the dictates of his body.

Upon achieving enlightenment, however, the Buddha renounced both of these extremes. Implicit in this is a rejection of the common understanding that mind and body were separate and that spirituality required the mortification of the body in order to free the mind. Sitting under the Bodhi Tree, he realized that a strong and healthy body is a prerequisite for profound insight and spiritual awakening. Body and mind must work together toward enlightenment. The Buddha's way of life was the result of his effort to focus on regimes of mind-body training that would eliminate the greed, hatred, and delusion that negatively affect most people's lives.

Although he no doubt spent considerable time in the solitude of meditation, the Buddha was fully engaged with other people of all kinds. As the number of his followers grew rapidly, he would have spent time instructing them, organizing them, and dealing with the wide range of issues that would have arisen among them. As his career developed, he spent more and more time in urban areas, where he would encounter potential disciples among all classes, from the wealthy nobles to the working class who farmed the land or labored in other industries. At least for the Buddha himself, Buddhism was far from a life of isolation and disengagement. His own life demonstrated how one might be an active participant in the larger social world while still maintaining meditative and contemplative wisdom. Since the Buddha's teachings weren't primarily about other worlds or divine beings but about the most pressing issues of human life, there was no place to be but among the people.

1.7. Who were the early disciples of the Buddha, and what kinds of lives did they live?

Because Buddhist teachings and practices focus so resolutely on the alleviation of suffering, it would be natural to assume that its appeal was strongest among the lower classes, whose scarce resources must have produced the greatest suffering. But this appears not to have been the case. Town and urban dwellers, landowners, members of the upper two castes, business people, and what the early texts refer to as those from "respectable families" were well represented among the Buddha's early disciples. That they were willing to renounce their wealth and status is a sign of the charisma of the Buddha and the appeal of his teachings. Becoming a Buddhist was increasingly popular among people in all walks of life. Among the Buddha's early disciples were Kaundinya, the first of the five ascetics to awaken under the Buddha's influence; Ananda, the Buddha's cousin and a disciple renowned for his capacity to remember the Buddha's sermons, or sutras; and Shariputra, a close disciple whose understanding of the teachings was exemplary. Several members of the Buddha's own royal family converted to Buddhism, including the aunt who had raised him, the Buddha's own son, and his father.

Not everyone who was inspired to follow the Buddha embraced life as a wandering mendicant, however. Gradually, a nonmonastic lay following developed among people who wanted to follow Buddhist teachings and practices while remaining in their families and occupations. The distinction between lay and ordained Buddhists was essential to the success of Buddhism. Those who took vows of renunciation followed the life of the Buddha, while others chose to devote themselves to providing the substantial means necessary to maintain the monks and nuns in their life of unqualified meditative practice.

Until recently it was thought that Buddhist monasteries were a much later development. Evidence has mounted, however that monasteries appeared very early in the history of Buddhism, perhaps even within the Buddha's lifetime. Since the very beginning of Buddhism, it was the custom of monks and the Buddha himself to settle in a single place—caves or a protected forest—during the Indian monsoon season, when constant rain would have prevented travel. These periodic retreats may have seamlessly evolved into permanent monastic dwellings for monks who could have taken advantage of better conditions to improve their practices of meditation. In either case, those who left home in order to take refuge in the Buddha's way of life gradually helped him shape a diverse community of spiritual seekers called the sangha.

1.8. How did early Buddhists conceive of themselves as a community, or sangha?

The Buddha spent the second half of his life, perhaps as much as forty-five years, developing a system of training and a set of teachings, called the dharma, that would most effectively lead others toward the awakened life that he was living. It is clear from his teachings that he also understood that an institutional foundation would be needed to maintain this new way of life down through the ages. The sangha is that institution, the social and cultural foundation of Buddhism. It was designed specifically to be an ideal spiritual community, one that would optimize the conditions of life under which awakening might occur. Although the sangha was initially conceived as a closed community of support among monks and nuns who had renounced ordinary life to focus exclusively on spiritual awakening, it was also clear that it could not exist without the larger supporting network of ordinary lay citizens whose labor would provide the material foundations for a Buddhist culture. Members of the sangha renounced the comforts and pleasures of ordinary life—sexual intimacy, family, possessions, and all other nonspiritual concerns—while the laity committed themselves to sustaining this way of life as an option for anyone choosing it.

This was thought to be a mutually beneficial arrangement. Obviously, members of the monastic community could not continue their way of life without the full support of the society around them—support that would feed them, clothe them, and provide all the other essentials of daily life. Having renounced work as well as family connections, monks and nuns intentionally made themselves dependent on others who would not make the same act of renunciation. Their debt to the society around them was clear to everyone.

But so was the benefit that monks and nuns would provide in exchange. The sangha was to be the exemplary moral standard of the society, a group of people who dedicated their lives to living as close to the Buddhist ideal as they could manage. To maintain this standard, Buddhist monks and nuns followed an elaborate code of discipline that laid out in considerable detail what an ideal life would look like. A significant portion of the Buddhist practice of mindfulness was the development of attention to these ideal guidelines for daily life. Moreover, this monastic discipline was designed as an expression of the mental qualities of unselfishness and compassion for others. It was very clear to members of the early Buddhist sangha that their very existence depended on the reputation that their members had in the society.

It is worth mentioning that occasionally the word *sangha* has been used more broadly to refer to the community of all Buddhists, including everyone who identifies as Buddhist, whether monastic or lay. This was not its original meaning, however, and it remains to be seen how this important Buddhist word and concept will develop in the future.

1.9. What was the role of women in the early Buddhist community?

The widespread assumption in the Buddha's time and place, as well as almost everywhere else in the world, was that religious matters were exclusively the domain of men. There appear to have been no exceptions. Yet in spite of this long-standing assumption, the Buddha instituted an order of nuns very early on and in doing so embarked upon a radical religious and social experiment. Buddhist texts tell how the Buddha's aunt and stepmother wanted to engage in the Buddhist quest and that they asked Ananda, the Buddha's cousin and closest disciple, to make this request of the Buddha. The Buddha is described as having been initially reluctant, worried that the inclusion of women would undermine the vow of celibacy that he took to be essential to fully engaged spiritual life. Nevertheless, he agreed to the request on the condition that special rules would maintain the monastic community's separation between men and women and that Buddhist nuns would be officially subordinate to monks in matters of decision-making. Nuns were required to honor monks as their seniors; the two groups lived separately; and nuns were subject to criticism from monks, but not the other way around.

These restrictive policies were not a reflection of an official Buddhist position on the religious inferiority of women, however. Most Buddhist texts hold that both men and women are capable of attaining the highest state of enlightenment. In an important early document, the *Therigata*, women are recognized as having achieved enlightenment to the same extent as monks, and there are stories in which the Buddha himself acknowledges the enlightenment of women. These early, liberating developments opened possibilities for women that had not been available before, in India or elsewhere. They created a vocation for women outside of home and family that made advancement, recognition, and achievement real possibilities. Although this didn't change the fact that all Buddhist cultures maintained patriarchal customs and traditions, it opened doors for women that had been fully closed.

It is overwhelmingly the case, however, that the central texts of Buddhism were written by men. And so it should not be surprising that issues tended to be framed in relation to men and, occasionally, that misogynist views emerge. One text goes so far as to proclaim that a female Buddha is not even possible. The long history of Buddhism shows the difficulties of establishing real gender equality within cultural traditions that were and are strongly patriarchal. Nevertheless, change in the status of women is clearly under way in virtually every Buddhist community in the world, and these changes suggest that there may well be a fundamental transformation of Buddhism in the twenty-first century.

1.10. What were the rules that governed the lives of monks and nuns?

The Buddha had summarized the path to awakening in terms of its three essential components: morality, meditation, and wisdom. Although the first of these—morality—entails a profound and equally distributed compassion for all living beings, it was recognized that in order to imagine this state and to strive toward it, a clear set of guidelines would be important. Every monk and nun who joined the sangha needed specific practices that would help cultivate this inner moral concern and a set of indicators that would tell him or her what to do and what not to do in order to fulfill the ideals of the Buddhist path. To satisfy this need, early Buddhists produced the *Vinaya*, the oldest code of monastic discipline in the world. We don't know when this code was written down, but the issues that it raises and the rules it stipulates must have gone all the way back to include the Buddha's own guidance. The text of the *Vinaya* is now one of three types of Buddhist sacred text that also includes the Buddhist sutras and early Buddhist elaboration or commentary on important issues in the sutras (the *Abhidharma*), both of which will be discussed below.

The *Vinaya* appears to be the product of monks and nuns debating among themselves about how exactly to live in accordance with the ideal of Buddhist enlightenment. This code stipulates in some detail what to do and what not to do in as many circumstances as they could imagine at that time. Guiding principles are evident throughout. Having dedicated their lives to enlightenment, it was clear that monks and nuns should live as simply as possible, with minimal possessions and few social and familial obligations, while at the same time fulfilling the Buddha's Middle Path between self-indulgence and self-mortification. The rules were formulated to help aspiring Buddhists maintain the conviction that nothing should distract them from the pursuit of awakening. While encouraging adherence to these rules of moral conduct in a strict discipline of mindfulness, the *Vinaya* also warns against becoming rigidly rule-bound and moralistic.

One of the significant issues addressed in the *Vinaya* is ordination, procedures stipulating who can become a monk or nun and how. Ordination takes place in two stages. Anyone eight years or older can "go forth" from ordinary life into the monastic life by formally requesting that a senior monk in good standing become his or her teacher and guide. Then, in a ritual of admittance, each novice has his or her head shaved and is given a robe. Novices then recite an ancient Buddhist formula, committing themselves to take spiritual refuge in "the Buddha, the dharma, and the sangha" (the Buddha, his teachings, and his community of followers). There are ten training rules to which monks and nuns vow commitment: (1) to refrain from harming living beings, (2) to refrain from stealing, (3) to refrain from sexual activity, (4) to refrain from lying, (5) to refrain from intoxicants, (6) to refrain from eating after midday, (7) to refrain from all entertainments, (8) to refrain from wearing jewelry or perfume, (9) to refrain from sleeping on luxurious beds, and (10) to refrain from handling money.

The second stage of ordination requires applicants to be at least twenty years of age and a suitable representative of the Buddhist sangha in a variety of ways. Having met these criteria the ordination candidate must participate in a ceremony in which at least five fully ordained monks are present. The new monk or nun vows to live in accordance with the *Vinaya*; to maintain a shaved head and wear monastic robes; to renounce ordinary family life, including all sexuality; and to live without an occupation or means of livelihood and without possessions other than a robe, a razor, and a begging bowl (although details of this list vary). The candidate vows to live by the generosity of others and to maintain full-time pursuit of enlightenment. Monks and nuns are still recognizable today by their shaved heads and monastic robes. Without hair and with body shapes obscured by loose-fitting robes, gender differentiation virtually disappears. Robe colors differ from culture to culture: they are orange or brown in Southeast Asia, gray or black in East Asia, and maroon in Tibetan areas.

Following ordination ceremonies, one becomes a full Buddhist monk or nun whose life is regulated by elaborate rules of demeanor. These rules vary from version to version and from culture to culture but tend to fall between 225 and 260 in number. Infractions against the rules may result in probation or even expulsion. Rules are weighed in terms of their importance, such that breaking a central rule regarding harming others or sexual abstinence may result in being expelled from the sangha. Other, less significant infractions result in lighter forms of reprimand. Although the code of discipline does stipulate who is entitled to judge or administer punishment for these offenses, there is no administrative or political hierarchy for the sangha. The Buddha explained to his disciples that after his death, no leader would need to be named. From that point on, Buddhists would receive their guidance directly from the teachings (dharma) and the code of discipline (*Vinaya*). Consensus among senior participants became the final mode of decision-making.

1.11. What was the relationship between members of the monastic community and lay Buddhists?

Although members of the earliest sangha must have conceived of themselves as renouncing ordinary society in order to pursue a wholehearted, disciplined form of spiritual achievement, it must also have become clear very early that monks' and nuns' relation to the rest of society was crucial. And so it has been throughout the history of Buddhism. The laity and early Indian political regimes regarded the Buddhist sangha as the moral and spiritual foundation of their society. Its contribution came to be regarded as essential to the social fabric. Early texts make the reciprocal relationship explicit. Householders were to provide gifts of material goods necessary for a life of meditation, and in return monks and nuns would provide the "gift of the dharma," becoming the teachers and models of moral conduct for the society.

Indeed, the code of conduct for monks and nuns, the *Vinaya*, requires that they proceed into the nearby village every day in order to receive these gifts of food directly. In addition, beyond communicating Buddhist teachings, monks and nuns were expected to participate in important events in the village: marriages, funerals, the dedication of new buildings, and so on. In return, the householders would seek to fulfill their obligation of generosity and support for the sangha. These reciprocal exchanges didn't always or necessarily imply any final commitment to Buddhism on the part of the laity. Religious pluralism in India, as elsewhere in Asia, often meant that gifts could be given to very different religious groups. But over time, no doubt, commitments must have developed both in families and in villages as a whole.

The Buddhist lay community did make a commitment specifically to Buddhism when they formally recited the "three refuges," declaring that they would "take refuge" throughout their lives "in the Buddha, the dharma, and the sangha." These men and women were encouraged to commit themselves to five basic precepts, which they would recite along with the "three refuges," making a commitment to (1) refrain from harming living beings, (2) refrain from taking what does not belong to them, (3) refrain from sexual misconduct, (4) refrain from various forms of false speech, and (5) refrain from intoxicants.

1.12. What kinds of religious involvement were available to the lay community?

The central concept for lay religious practice was the "merit" to be gained for oneself, one's family, and one's society through wholesome and auspicious activities. A meritorious action is one generating good karma that would come to fruition either now or sometime in the future. This kind of merit came in three broad categories: generosity, virtuous conduct, and meditation. Householders were counseled to be diligent in work, moderate in their expenditures, and constructive members of their communities, with special attention to maintaining the sangha with generous donations.

The second category of merit, virtue or moral conduct, entailed adherence to the five precepts listed above. Virtuous living was thus one form of religious practice. Lay people who wanted to go further in these moral practices while still retaining their lay status were encouraged to follow eight of the ten precepts governing the lives of monks and nuns. Often this practice would be followed for a specified period of time and would entail sexual abstinence (rather than avoidance of sexual misconduct), refraining from eating after midday, refraining from all entertainments and from wearing jewelry or perfume, and refraining from sleeping on luxurious beds. Adopting these more arduous disciplines put lay Buddhists on a path of spiritual attainment similar to that of monks and nuns if only for a limited period of time.

The third category of religious practice for the laity was meditation. It was assumed throughout the history of Buddhism, however, that few householders would have the time or patience to pursue this practice in depth. Rudimentary instructions in contemplative practice were given to the laity, but early Buddhist writings show that these were minimal. Nevertheless, anyone wishing to pursue this highest form of religious practice could receive instruction from monks and nuns.

Because complete enlightenment was reserved for monks and nuns, lay Buddhists began to think in terms of gradual advancement in life or in many lives. In this sense, common people would engage in acts of generosity, virtue, and perhaps some effort at meditation in order to awaken to a life of wisdom and compassion or in hopes of a better rebirth. It is unclear from the earliest Buddhist texts what level of spiritual achievement the Buddha and other Buddhists thought might be possible for serious lay practitioners, but the assumption was that with sufficient discipline and dedication at least some exalted states of character might be attained.

1.13. How did early Buddhists align themselves with the northern Indian social system, especially the early stages of the Indian caste system?

The earliest Buddhist monks were marginal to cultures of the villages through which they passed. Indeed, Buddhism offered a way out of that social system. Early northern Indian Vedic culture was led by a Brahman class that defined the religious obligations for human beings. For Buddhists, none of that mattered—neither the gods who were honored nor their required rituals nor the priests who conducted them. The Buddha argued against the dominant four-caste system of social division and allowed everyone, regardless of class, to join the sangha. "Not by birth is one elite or lowly, but by actions," the Buddha is reported to have said.

This is not to say, however, that the Buddha sought widespread social reform. In most respects the Buddha accepted the cultural status quo of his time. But within the Buddhist sangha, new and revolutionary rules would be in effect, and spiritual meritocracy was a fundamental part of that system. Individual achievement was based on karma and merit, and what was most important in determining the quality of an act was the intention behind it. If the intention behind an enormous gift was primarily self-serving, and the intention behind a poor person's small gift was profoundly selfless, then the latter would be spiritually superior to the former. This idea altered the outlook of early Buddhists in significant ways and made traditional class divisions look artificial and unnecessary.

Yet on cultural and political matters in society at large, a restrained and at times conservative posture seems to have prevailed in early Buddhism. The Buddha, like Jesus, had nothing critical to say about slavery, for example. Slavery was a long-standing and widespread institution prior to the modern world and for the most part went without comment from religious leaders in virtually every tradition. Social reform was not the purpose of the Buddhist sangha nor of Buddhist teachings. But within the sangha a set of revolutionary religious norms would prevail.

1.14. What are the sacred texts of Buddhism?

Buddhist sacred writings are divided into three types, collectively called the *tripitaka*, or "three baskets": the "basket of discipline" (*vinaya*), the "basket of discourses" (sutras), and the "basket of further teachings" (*abhidharma*). The second of these, the sutras, is the largest and most important. *Sutras* (in the Sanskrit version) or *suttas* (in the Pali language) are purported to be records of talks or sermons given by the Buddha in a variety of settings.

Sutras are readily recognizable by their initial lines; they always begin with the same phrases: "Thus have I heard. At one time the Buddha was resident in such and such a location and was in the company of this or that group of people." Then they tell us what the Buddha taught those people on that occasion. The one who witnessed these gatherings and who later communicated what the Buddha had to say was Ananda, the Buddha's cousin and closest disciple.

It is important to recognize, however, that the custom at that time was for religious and philosophical teachings to be communicated in verbal rather than written form. What was remembered on these occasions was memorized by monks and nuns, taught to others, and then passed down to another generation of monastic memorizers. Although it is probable that some of these were written over the subsequent centuries, the Buddhist canon of sutras as a whole wasn't recorded in writing until the first century BCE, several hundred years after the death of the Buddha. No doubt some of these texts were altered over time; various cultural accommodations and other "improvements" would probably have been introduced without anyone noticing. The sutras do display consistency in their teachings and are written in a distinctive style, and we know that the standards for accuracy in memorization at that time were very high. Nevertheless, it is easy to see that strong historical claims about what the Buddha really said on some particular occasion almost two and a half millennia ago would be difficult to justify. Although perhaps important to intellectuals today, these issues of historical authenticity had no substantial bearing on the fundamental influence that Buddhist sutras have had on the tradition.

"Sacred texts" hold a very different position in Buddhism than do those in Western religions: the Hebrew Bible, the Christian Bible, and the Muslim Qur'an. Part of this difference has to do with the fact that in Buddhism there are just so many of them—more in fact than any one person can master. The Pali canon—the early sutras in the Pali language, just a subset of the whole—contain hundreds of sutras that in modern printed versions run to over fifty volumes. And although to some extent there is a "core" of sutras that constitutes a common heritage for all Buddhists, each form of Buddhism came to adopt its own version of the Buddhist canon, and for the most part this hasn't troubled Buddhists in the history of their interactions.

It is also the case that sutras went on being composed for many centuries and in several different languages. The sutras in the Pali canon are the ones most likely to deliver something close to what the Buddha might have taught. But that doesn't mean that these are the most influential or most authoritative texts in the full scope of the Buddhist tradition. Still, these early sutras give us a distinctive glimpse into the epoch of the founder of Buddhism. These texts are arranged into four collections based on their length: long, midlength, and two short sutra collections. All of these have been translated into English and are readily available for interesting, if difficult reading. They are highly repetitious, use distinct figures of speech, and are full of numerical lists—all to aid those tasked with memorizing them. What they give us, though, is a wonderful picture of the Buddha and his close disciples, full of intriguing stories about the kinds of lives they lived. They abound in humor, poetry, legend, and irony and are one of the great collections of early human literature.

1.15. What issues do the early Buddhist sutras address, and how were these texts used in practice?

The earliest Buddhist sutras are relatively brief, perhaps what we should expect from a memory-based account of a talk that may have gone on for an hour or so. The brevity of the sutras helped facilitate memorization and would also have suited the highly diverse audiences to whom they were taught. But the range of issues they address is anything but limited. The Buddha lived for as many as forty-five years after his enlightenment and traveled constantly from village to village to give talks. He addressed everyone from children to elders and from the poorest to the wealthiest and most prominent citizens. On occasion he spoke before kings and nobles, sometimes to criminals, even to some who threatened him with violence. Sometimes the sutras show him in debate with rival teachers, and on these occasions we get glimpses of what is distinct about Buddhism.

There were times of famine, times of prosperity, times of political turmoil and of overall well-being. The sutras have the Buddha speaking to virtually every issue that was of pressing concern: death and disease, wealth and poverty, virtue and corruption, and the very nature of human existence. There were family issues, issues that pertained only to celibate monks and nuns, and very particular issues that perplexed whatever group he happened to be visiting. If his teachings were to pass the test of relevancy in each of these settings, answers to questions in all of these arenas of real life had to be persuasively provided. But interwoven into all of these diverse topics were the central concerns of the dharma: understanding the persistence of human suffering and learning effective, enlightened ways of living in light of it.

Once a somewhat standard set of talks or sermons had been established—sutras that the Buddha probably repeated on numerous occasions—these could be used by his closest and most trustworthy disciples as the topics for discourse whenever the Buddha himself wasn't around. As Buddhism grew, some monks wandered or lived separately from the Buddha but would present sutra talks in a manner that sought to emulate him. And of course after the death of the Buddha, the teachings of Buddhism continued to be communicated in this same form through the memorization efforts of many subsequent Buddhists. Thus the sutras were the primary vehicles through which Buddhist teachings were transmitted. For monks and nuns this would have entailed rigorous efforts at memorization, and for everyone the primary issue was how to apply these teachings to specific issues in everyday life in order to be able to live in a distinctively Buddhist way.

1.16. What was the relationship between Buddhism and other Indian religious traditions in this early period?

Early India, like most other places in the world at that time, was the home of many different local languages and cultures.

Every area would have had its own distinct traditions and ways of living. These differences were often linguistic—each area with its own language or dialect, making communication difficult, if not impossible. These differences included religion. Indeed, as far as we know early Indians had no separate word for *religion* and therefore no concept that matches our modern word. Religious practices, customs, and beliefs blended in with all the other practices, customs, and beliefs that sustained these cultures. By the early centuries of Buddhism, we can see the development of widely shared tendencies that transcended certain cultural and linguistic differences.

Because they inhabited the same geographical space, competition between religious groups must have been significant. Although we see little evidence of violent responses to these differences—no wars that appeared to be primarily religious in character—there were clearly debates and arguments. Evidence for this can be seem in the Buddhist sutras, where the Buddha is pictured debating with a Brahman or criticizing an alternative belief or practice. Buddhism wasn't conceived along limited cultural lines as the religion of this or that particular ethnic group, and as a result of this universality, Buddhists were interested in persuading new groups of people to join. The Buddha himself had taught followers that the awakening of character and culture they advocated should be offered to all individuals and all groups, and that spreading the dharma was one form of compassionate spiritual practice. So even though we don't know much about this, we can safely imagine serious debate and competition between religious options in early India.

1.17. When and how did the Buddha die?

By the end of his life, around the age of eighty, the Buddha was well known and highly regarded in northern India. After more than four decades of teaching, the Buddha was suffering the effects of old age that he had pondered as a young prince. The

Buddhist sangha had been carefully organized; the dharma, or teachings, had been articulated, clarified, and honed; and as a consequence the Buddha had come to regard his task as complete. A sutra depicting the end of his life claims that the Buddha told his followers he would live another three months. During this time, he attempted to provide a simple summary of the teachings and practices of Buddhism in the form of multiple lists of essentials, now a text common to all Buddhists, called *The Wings to Awakening*.

The Buddha also addressed the always troublesome question of succession: Who would be in charge of the sangha? Claiming that no one had ever been in charge, he dismissed the need for a "successor" and said that the teachings and the rules for monks and nuns would be sufficient to guide the conscience of every individual. Lacking a central authority, Buddhists would encourage everyone to follow their own conscience. Indeed, at that time this organization wasn't called Buddhism. The Buddha taught the dharma, certainly not a devotional religion focused on himself.

The Buddha's final meal was given at the home of a blacksmith named Cunda, but something in it—either tainted meat or poisonous mushrooms—began to cause him great intestinal pain. Walking through this pain some distance to the town of Kushinagar, the Buddha sat in meditation between two trees. He gave burial instructions: he was to be cremated and his remains enshrined in a stone burial mound, or *stupa*. Asking his followers if there were any final questions, the stunned disciples are reported to have responded with nothing but tearful sadness. Reiterating the most crucial point of the dharma, the Buddha then spoke his last words: "All conditioned things are impermanent. Pursue your awakening with discipline."

One who has lived in a state of nirvana is said at death to pass into a condition of *parinirvana*, nirvana beyond life. The Buddhist texts describing this momentous event, written several hundred years after its occurrence, claim that earthquakes and thunder marked the occasion as world-historical in significance, just as had been the case for the Buddha's birth and enlightenment. And indeed, that it was of world-historical significance turned out to be true. Although we have no way to say how many Buddhists there were at the time of the founder's death, as billions of followers in dozens of nations later shaped their lives in terms of his teachings, we can say with some confidence that no more historically significant human being has ever lived.

1.18. What happened to the Buddhist community following the death of the Buddha?

The death of a founder and visionary leader is a major transition, one that might easily portend the decline or end of a group. We know a little about how this crucial transition occurred in Buddhism. First, a council was convened, the first of several that would be called in the centuries to follow. This initial meeting was held in the area of Rajagraha during the first three-month rainy season after the Buddha had passed away. The five hundred leading Buddhists, those who were regarded as *arhats*, awakened monks, gathered to test the extent of their agreement on the content of the dharma and the *Vinaya*. Did they share a view of what the Buddha's teachings really meant, and did they share an understanding of the details of monastic life required to realize that meaning? Ananda is reported to have begun by reciting the sutras from memory. "Thus have I heard," he would say, over and over in moving from one sutra to another as he recalled what he had heard the Buddha teach.

There are no writings dating from this period, so it is not at all clear how much these later texts really do capture the tenor of that historical event. And the confusion amid differences of opinion must have already been substantial. Individuals were allowed to recite the sutras in their own language and dialect. In fact, today it isn't certain which dialects the Buddha himself spoke, although the Pali language in which these texts are best preserved must have been very close to the original. In any case, it would be difficult to imagine complete agreement about what it was all the arhats had learned from the Buddha, especially since the Buddha was well-known to practice an impressive degree of rhetorical flexibility in teaching each person and group in accordance with their needs and capacities. Still, enough agreement emerged from that huge gathering that Buddhism would be able to thrive in the decades and centuries to follow.

Buddhism grew and grew rapidly in northern India. Senior members of the sangha traveled in all directions, residing temporarily in village after village and city upon city. They must have impressed their hosts since residents continued to offer them sustenance and a place to sleep, hoping to hear in exchange what these visitors had to say about how best to live an awakened life. It also appears that commercial and political powers must have regarded Buddhism as a valuable asset. Monks were well-organized, were sworn to poverty and humility, and aspired to lead moral lives that would be admirable in any social setting. They helped calm and pacify communities that had been torn by war or disagreement, and this stable social environment would have seemed conducive and beneficial to the expanding mercantile economies that were developing. The Buddha himself had strong relationships with several monarchs and political leaders, and records tell us that most of these were deeply impressed with what Buddhism offered their communities.

This connection between Buddhism and political power came to fruition when, in 268 BCE, Emperor Ashoka came to the throne as the third ruler in the powerful Mauryan dynasty established by his grandfather. Although a warrior like his predecessors, several years into his reign Ashoka was said to have great remorse at the killing that had brought him to power. Having been impressed with the calm peacefulness of

Buddhist monks, he decided to become a Buddhist himself and to encourage others in his empire to do the same. Ashoka sent out emissaries to teach Buddhism to cultures as far west as the Mediterranean and as far south as Sri Lanka. A new world religion was born.

2

BUDDHIST DIVERSITY

2.1. How and when did Buddhism spread beyond its origins in northeastern India?

Buddhism began expanding out from its birthplace during the Buddha's life, and that process continues today. Its mode of dissemination has typically been word of mouth: from person to person and community to community in one form or another. As we have seen, the Buddha and his disciples wandered by foot throughout the northern Indian plains, settling into a village for long enough to leave a favorable impression of lives intent on nonviolence, moral discipline, and wisdom—and then moving on to the next village. For centuries monks and nuns followed this nomadic life before gradually shifting to the settled life of Buddhist monasteries. Even then, however, Buddhist monks were to be found walking through virtually every region of India, and eventually beyond India into the rest of Asia. Buddhism reached the island of Sri Lanka by the third century BCE and quickly established that nation as the exemplary Buddhist culture that it remains today. Perhaps as early as Emperor Ashoka's missions in the third century BCE, Buddhist emissaries began traveling east into Southeast Asia, beginning in what today would be Bangladesh and Myanmar and over centuries eventually extending into Thailand, Cambodia, Laos, and Vietnam as well as down the peninsula into present-day Malaysia, Singapore, and Indonesia.

Buddhist monks transported Buddhist teachings to the west and north as well, crossing northern India into the Indus River Valley, through what is now Pakistan and into the mountainous regions of Afghanistan. Although these are strongly Islamic areas today, centuries ago they were equally strong Buddhist cultures, as was vividly evident when in 2001 the Taliban destroyed enormous fourth- and fifth-century images of the Buddha carved into the stone mountainside in the Bamiyan Valley in Afghanistan. Although traces of a Buddhist presence can be found even further to the west—as far as the Mediterranean—these travelers were guests whose arrival did not lead to substantial Buddhist cultures there. To the north Buddhist monks were found throughout Central Asia. Running east to west just north of Pakistan and Afghanistan, the Silk Road took Buddhist travelers to Uzbekistan, Tajikistan, Kyrgyzstan, Kazakhstan, and beyond, where Buddhism has long been an influential part of these cultures.

To the Far East, Buddhist monks were seen in northern China in the first century of the Common Era, and over the next few centuries China adopted Buddhism alongside its Confucian and Daoist heritages. From China Buddhism quickly found its way into Korea, Mongolia, Japan, and down into Vietnam again. And by the seventh and eighth centuries, Buddhism was entering Tibet from all directions. Although these are the nations that have traditionally been associated with Buddhism, the list continues to expand today as Buddhist temples, monasteries, and meditation centers can now be found in every major city in every country in the world. All of these conversions and extensions of Buddhist culture appear to have occurred very slowly and gradually through persuasive writings, talks, conversations, and the influence of exemplary lives.

2.2. What are the primary sectarian divisions within Buddhism, and how did they develop?

Diversity appears to have been inscribed into the character of Buddhism from the very beginning. The Buddha taught the dharma to a wide range of people, from youth to the aged, from the wealthy to the impoverished, and from one culture to another. To different audiences he is reported to have offered different advice, depending on the issues they faced. And as he taught for as many as forty-five years, that range must have been extensive. It should not be surprising, then, that different orientations to Buddhism would develop in order to accommodate these differences in background and context.

Although accounts of the first Buddhist council, written long after the event itself, do not reveal the range and diversity of views that must surely have been voiced, the very need for a meeting to agree on a core vision of the dharma points to the existence of these differences. One century later, a second council was convened precisely because differences in the ways monks and nuns were engaged in their practices began to be noticeable and to some degree problematic. These differences were first of all geographical: monks in eastern India had come to understand the demands of the monastic code (*Vinaya*) somewhat differently from monks in the west. In this case their discussions couldn't bring them to agreement, yielding the first sectarian division in Buddhism (between the Elders and the Great Assembly). Differences in location and setting also tend to indicate differences in dialect and culture, and over thousands of years of Buddhist history it is this factor of geographical and cultural separation that best accounts for the significant range of ways of being Buddhist.

Although there were a number of different schools of thought that emerged in the first four centuries of Buddhist history, one division over time became the single most important distinction within Buddhism. This is the distinction, emerging just prior to the beginning of the Common Era, between Theravada Buddhism, sometimes called Southern Buddhism or Hinayana Buddhism, and Mahayana Buddhism, or Northern Buddhism. Although we will clarify the differences in teachings and practices between these two kinds of Buddhism later, at this point their geographical and cultural differences are most important. The Theravada school of Buddhism is the one that has flourished throughout Southeast Asia, in Myanmar, Thailand, Laos, and Cambodia, as well as in Sri Lanka.

Related to the Elders represented at the first two Buddhist councils, Theravada Buddhists managed to preserve the entire *Tripitaka*—the "three baskets" of sacred texts—in the Pali language. Pali is therefore the classical language that guides the study of the dharma in these Southeast Asian cultures and that unites them in common Theravada Buddhist teachings and practices. The Elders, as we might surmise, tended to be conservative in orientation, seeking to preserve Buddhism as the Buddha himself taught it. The name *Hinayana*, which is sometimes used to designate this form of Buddhism, originated as a pejorative term, one that implied a lesser status, and is therefore to be used advisedly, if at all.

Mahayana or Northern Buddhism began to emerge as a distinctive voice and as a new form of sutra literature as early as the first century BCE. Although this form of Buddhism began in India and seems to have been particularly strong in certain regions (western and southern India), it also spread outward from India in all directions. To the west Mahayana Buddhism flourished for centuries in current-day Pakistan and Afghanistan. Moving northwest from the northern Indian plains Mahayana Buddhism spread through Kashmir into virtually all Central Asian cultures along the Silk Road, where today it is still prevalent in Tibet and Mongolia. And to the east Mahayana was absorbed in China, Korea, Japan, and Vietnam, where it remains today the dominant form of Buddhism.

Within this primary division of Buddhism into Theravada and Mahayana, other subdivisions have arisen, some historically important and others less significant. We will refer to these wherever a basic understanding of Buddhism requires it. There is one further separation, however, that should be mentioned now: at some point in the development of Mahayana Buddhism a distinct tendency arose that warranted a new name, the Vajrayana. Although closely tied to the Mahayana, Vajrayana adds a new set of Tantric ideas and practices that

Buddhist Diversity 39

give it a distinct flavor. This form of Buddhism is today practiced primarily in Tibet and Mongolia.

2.3. What are the distinguishing characteristics of Buddhism in the Southeast Asian cultures of Myanmar, Thailand, Laos, and Cambodia, and how are these Buddhist cultures linked to Buddhist traditions in Sri Lanka?

These cultures have for many centuries been the stronghold of traditional Theravada Buddhism, the form favored by the Elders in the early tradition and the one that is best known for the effort to preserve the tradition as it was handed down from the Buddha himself. Buddhism first appeared in Sri Lanka in the third century BCE and underwent steady assimilation through the many centuries that followed. Buddhism began its migration into Southeast Asia at roughly the same time, purportedly under the missionary zeal of Emperor Ashoka, although this was probably limited to the western sections of what was once called Indo-China due to its location between the two massive civilizations of India and China.

For many centuries, the Buddhism that existed in Southeast Asian cultures was a diverse mix of all known forms of Buddhism: Mahayana and Vajrayana, along with the Theravada traditions that eventually came to dominate. These Buddhist traditions were shaped by the influences of Hindu Brahmanical religious tendencies and native animistic cults that had developed long before the influx of Buddhism. The eventual ascendency of Theravada Buddhism was due in part to its capacity to absorb rather than reject religious beliefs and practices that originated in these other traditions.

In each of these countries Buddhism provided the religious foundations for the development from small, subsistence-level villages into the larger, coherent economies and cultures that we find in Southeast Asia today. Rulers in these cultures were attracted to Theravada Buddhism for the moral legitimation it provided and for the assistance it could offer toward establishing social harmony and integration. The Buddhist sangha managed to maintain a reputation for integrity and disciplined life, and this trait was attractive to the cultural elite and helped exert moral pressure on rulers to govern for the benefit of the common people as well as the aristocrats.

Each of these Southeast Asian Theravada Buddhist cultures is characterized by a firm division between two sectors: the monastic sangha and the laity. Lay Buddhists worked to provide economic and political stability but looked up to monks and nuns for the kinds of moral and religious guidance that would unite the culture. This division was carefully maintained, and each group helped keep the other from harmful forms of excess. Basic to Theravada Buddhism is the pursuit of religious merit through three means: generosity, virtue, and meditation. Generosity was primarily the task of the laity, who would provide the means of support for the sangha. Meditation was the primary responsibility of the sangha, although lay meditation practice was always a possibility, even if rarely adopted. And both were responsible for the third merit-making practice— virtue—in spite of the fact that the virtues necessary to be a good mother or ruler or farmer were in certain respects different from those characteristic of a good monk or nun.

Although each of these cultures evolved over time in their own ways, their unity has been effectively maintained through their mutual adoption of Theravada Buddhism.

2.4. What are Mahayana sutras, and how are they different from earlier texts associated with the Buddha?

Although some forms of reading and writing had been practiced among scribes and the elite in South Asia for well over a millennium, the two-century historical period from roughly 100 BCE to 100 CE is generally thought to be the turning point when a predominantly oral culture became a sophisticated literary culture. The earliest Buddhist sutras that have come down to us in written form show several important signs of oral culture. They are brief, simple sermons attributed to the Buddha and amenable to memorization. Highly repetitious, with distinct figures of speech and full of numerical lists, these texts passed from one monk or nun to another through focused repetition and internalization. Accessible to a broad audience, these texts were the basis of Buddhist teachings and the engine driving the spread of Buddhism throughout South Asia. As the Common Era approached, however, the advent of a new literary trend in India made it inevitable that these oral practices would gradually give way to writing, and this transition no doubt occurred somewhat unnoticeably over several centuries.

In the wake of this transition from oral to written culture, beginning in the first century BCE Buddhist sutras of a different kind began to be written and to circulate among literate Buddhists. Although these sutras began with the well-known phrase "Thus have I heard," thereby purporting to be transcriptions of the Buddha's public talks, these texts were fundamentally different in format and were clearly products of the emerging literary culture rather than remnants from the time of the historical Buddha. These sutras were considerably longer, sometimes hundreds of pages rather than a dozen or so, and thus no longer easily memorized. They often demonstrated extravagant literary style and flair and sought to evoke a grand vision of the entire cosmos in Buddhist terms. The creative possibilities of cultural evolution had now put Buddhism into an environment of rapid development and expansion.

The earliest of these Mahayana sutras, the *Perfection of Wisdom* sutras, were disseminated throughout South Asia and featured a distinction between at least two kinds of Buddhism. Criticizing the limitations of earlier Buddhism, the new sutras claimed to represent a Mahayana, a "great vehicle" that would lead to full Buddhahood for all sentient beings, in contrast to the "small vehicle" (Hinayana) aspirations that they claimed were being taught by the elder disciples. Surprisingly, however, practitioners of both schools continued to live together in the same monasteries and with the same moral and ritual practices. Nevertheless, a growing rift in Buddhist styles had taken hold and would develop further as Buddhism was disseminated throughout Asia. Distinctively Mahayana sutras continued to be written for at least seven centuries, adding substantial volume to the category of Buddhist scripture.

2.5. How many sutras are there, and to what extent do Buddhists read them?

There are more than five thousand sutras that have come down to us in the Pali language, all of which purport to be remembered transcriptions of talks given by the Buddha during his roughly forty-five-year teaching career. In Chinese translations of the Pali, there are even more, and many of these have yet to be translated into any other language. Then, to complicate matters for the discerning Buddhist reader, there are also more than six hundred Mahayana sutras that have survived, mostly in Chinese or Tibetan, although a few Sanskrit originals have also survived. Some of these sutras are well over five hundred pages in length. It would be a good guess that a thousand or more texts purporting to be sutras have also been lost over long stretches of Buddhist history and transition. The sheer volume of Buddhist sacred literature is hard to grasp. This means that no one can seriously consider reading all of the Buddhist sutras available, today or at almost any point in earlier Buddhist history.

But of course, Buddhists do read and revere sutras as the original proclamation of their religion. How do they choose which ones to read, and which ones do they in fact choose? As in any other literary culture, reading choices tend to be made by way of recommendation, either by word of mouth or written commendation. Monks and nuns tend to read the sutras that their teachers valorized and taught to them, and the same is true for literate lay people. Moreover teachers tend to recommend those that were taught to them and that form the basis of their particular lineage of Buddhism. Which sutras come to the foreground depends on personal, cultural, sectarian, and historical circumstances. There are no sutras so universally revered and popular that they have been read by all Buddhists in all periods of Buddhist history.

From this brief description it should be clear that if we refer to sutras as Buddhist scripture, it would be important to recognize that the word *scripture* carries connotations borrowed from Western religions that don't fully apply in the case of Buddhism. The sheer volume and variety of these texts mean that reading preferences among different groups of Buddhists inevitably diverge rather widely. But the fact that one group doesn't recommend that a certain sutra be read has almost never meant that anyone in the group would deny that the text was the authentic word of the Buddha. Chinese, Korean, and Japanese Buddhists, for example, would never claim that the early Pali sutras weren't truly spoken by the Buddha even though it would almost never occur to them to read these sutras for spiritual guidance. Sutras are regularly read and often recited in ritual. But which ones are in play depends on which Buddhists are practicing in which historical period. Although the sutras are sacred texts, what that means in Buddhist terms is quite different from what it means to be a sacred text in Western religions.

2.6. Among these many Buddhist sutras, which ones are most important to read to get a good sense of Buddhist sacred texts?

Among the sutras that are widely read today and that would provide a solid foundation for understanding Buddhism, the following from the Pali or Theravada tradition would be well worth reading:

> The *Dhammacakkapavattana* sutra (*Setting the Dharma Wheel in Motion*) is regarded as the Buddha's first sermon after his enlightenment, given to his first disciples at the Deer Park in Sarnath.

The *Anattalakkhana* sutra, the Buddha's second discourse, provides basic instruction on the teachings of "impermanence" and "no self."

The *Aditta-pariyaya* sutra, widely known as the "Fire sutra," teaches about attachment, suffering, and liberation.

The *Chachakka* sutra gives the Buddha's meditation instructions on the purification of mind and the senses.

The *Satipatthāna* sutra and the *Mahāsatipatthāna* sutra are widely read sutras on the "four foundations of mindfulness" and other teachings crucial to the development of Buddhist meditation.

The *Ānāpānasati* sutra is the Buddha's basic meditation instruction on awareness of breathing.

The *Kalama* sutra is the Buddha's famous talk on free, nondogmatic inquiry as the basis of Buddhist practice.

The *Upanisa* sutra is the Buddha's first detailed teaching on causation, or "dependent arising."

All of these brief but important early Buddhist sutras are available online and in several of the translated collections of Pali sutras.

From the large collection of Mahayana sutras, these are among the most influential today:

The *Diamond* sutra and the *Heart* sutra are brief, encapsulated versions of the *Perfection of Wisdom* sutras that first develop the themes of the bodhisattva's practice of emptiness and compassion and the skillful means of living these insights.

The *Vimalakīrti* sutra tells the compelling story of a wealthy businessman who is nevertheless profoundly enlightened and skillful in his ability to live and to teach the Buddhist dharma.

The *Lotus* sutra, which became one of the central Buddhist texts in East Asia, tells an intriguing variety of stories that demonstrate the transcendent, divine character of the Buddha.

The *Avatamsaka* sutra is a voluminous meditation on the beauty and perfection of reality when seen from the enlightened perspective of total interdependence of all dimensions of reality.

The *Pure Land* sutras are the starting point for devotional Buddhism in India and Central Asia, but especially in China, Korea, and Japan.

All of these sutras are available in several modern language translations.

2.7. Besides the sutras, are there other Buddhist texts that have been equally influential in the development of Buddhism?

Indeed there are. First, it would be hard to overestimate the importance and historical impact of the *Vinaya*, the Buddhist code of conduct for monks and nuns. Because this code was traditionally considered to have been instituted and developed under the guidance of the Buddha himself in the earliest stages of the Buddhist sangha, and because this code determined virtually every detail of the life of those who would for centuries guide and shape the Buddhist tradition, this text, in several variations, has been highly influential. But there are many others. The *Jataka* tales are an intriguing collection of folk tales about who the Buddha was in his previous incarnations. The *Milindapanha*, a fascinating story about an encounter between a Buddhist monk and King Milinda (or Menander), has long been influential. Consider the *Mahavastu* (Great Story), a first-century CE account of the Buddha's life, and the *Buddhacarita* (Acts of the Buddha), a second-century CE poem telling the story of the life of the Buddha in compelling detail. There are also the *Dhammapada*, an extremely popular verse summary of sayings of the Buddha drawn from various sutras and addressing the central teachings of Buddhism; *Visuddhimagga* (Path of Purification), a classic statement of the teachings of Theravada Buddhism by the famous fifth century monk

Buddhaghosa; and, to name just one crucial Mahayana text, the *Mulamadhyamika karikas*, perhaps Buddhism's most famous philosophical text and one that helped launch the later development of Buddhist ideas.

These are just a few of the early writings of central importance. There would be many more as the cultures and epochs of Buddhism unfolded. Just as the writings of Augustine, Thomas Aquinas, and Martin Luther would have an enormous impact on the subsequent shape of Christianity, important Buddhist leaders in many historical epochs would help determine what Buddhism would come to be over time: Vasubhandu, Shantideva, Linji, Dogen, Shinran, Tsongkhapa, Thich Nhat Hanh, and Pema Chodron are just a few. Buddhist literature is staggeringly rich, not just in quantity but in the range of genres and styles, in the diverse issues addressed, and in the number of languages in which it has been written. This range and diversity continues to grow today as Buddhism settles into and absorbs the contributions of cultures all over the world.

2.8. Why and how is the Silk Road significant in Buddhist history?

Prior to the early centuries of Buddhist history, long-distance travel and trade moving east and west over the vast Eurasian landmass was extremely rare. The logistical difficulties of such travel were extreme. This terrain was marked by thousands of miles of barren landscape, mountains, high-elevation deserts, extremes of heat, cold, and wind, and very little water. The Silk Road began to be traveled perhaps as early as the third century BCE as a route through this treacherous wilderness, allowing skillful and daring travelers to navigate from one relatively dependable water source to another across the high-desert plateaus of Central Asia. Mastery of this treacherous trade route had the unintended consequence of setting up the conditions for the spread of Buddhism to regions thousands of miles from its original homeland.

The founding of the Central Asian Kusana Empire in the first century CE and its conversion to Buddhism meant that an enormous portion of the route—from northern India through Afghanistan and beyond—was under Buddhist influence. Buddhist culture spread westward during this period into Iran and the Greco-Roman world. Although by the ninth century the rise and spread of Islam would begin to undermine the position of Buddhism in these areas, its limited presence in some of these territories continues into the twenty-first century. While it was slower to develop, ultimately it would be the eastern stretch of the Silk Road that would be most transformative for Buddhism.

The very name we have given this Eurasian trade route indicates what, from a Western perspective, would have been most decisive: the movement westward of Chinese silks, which were valued above virtually all other commodities. The Silk Road was the initial route by which Buddhism would make its way in and out of China and the rest of East Asia, connecting China, Korea, and Japan to the other civilizations of the Eurasian world for the first time in human history. The significance of the Silk Road for the history of Buddhism is enormous, creating the conditions under which the Buddhist sphere of influence would stretch almost five thousand miles, from Tehran to Tokyo.

Although Islam has long been the dominant religious tradition along the Silk Road, and very few Buddhist temples and monuments remain on this vast stretch of high desert, there are a few exceptions to this pattern. The most notable of these are the Dunhuang Caves, located in an oasis area along the Silk Road in the far western region of Gansu, China, which provide hundreds of examples of Buddhist temple architecture and art that have been preserved for as many as 1,600 years. The most famous of these caves, the Mogao Caves, form a string of 492 temples carved into a desert hillside, some containing exquisite

examples of Buddhist painting and sculpture produced between the fourth and the fourteenth centuries. In 1900 a vast
collection of Buddhist sutras and other texts were discovered
in one of these caves, and the extensive repercussions of this
discovery for the understanding of Buddhist history have been
slowly coming to light ever since.

2.9. How was Buddhism introduced and assimilated into an already established and sophisticated Chinese culture?

The absorption of Buddhism into Chinese culture is one of the
most improbable and interesting developments in the entire
history of human cultural interaction. Although Buddhism
moved from its original Indian setting into many distinct
Asian cultures, in the case of China the adoption of Buddhism
occurred in an ancient culture that already had highly developed social, philosophical, and religious traditions. In spite
of its own sophistication and extensive cultural pride, and
given virtually perfect historical timing, China opened itself
to be profoundly influenced by all aspects of Indian Buddhist
culture: monastic organization, temple construction, religious ritual, views of death and the afterlife, philosophical inquiry, the concept of enlightenment, and meditation, as well
as artistic forms and styles of many kinds. At the same time,
gradual assimilation produced a unique synthesis of these two
ancient cultures, including varieties of Buddhist thought and
practice that had no precedent in India or elsewhere.

This unique historic assimilation occurred undramatically
and gradually over many centuries. The first historical
references to the presence of Buddhism in China are from the
first century CE. The first Buddhists in China were foreigners,
Central Asian merchants who had traveled the Silk Road to
do business in China, occasionally accompanied by Buddhist
monks whose presence was thought to help dissuade bandits
in the high-desert wilderness. By the second century CE these
merchants began to help establish Buddhist institutions in the

northern Chinese trading cities, at first most likely as refuges for themselves but as time went on also as centers that extended the influence of Buddhism into Chinese society.

The "perfect historical timing" referred to above was the gradual decline and then fall of the once prestigious Han dynasty in China. As Han political and social conditions worsened and as Buddhist ideas began to be translated and understood, the influence of Buddhism grew exponentially. When the government fell into chaotic dysfunction, the Confucian ideal of political engagement began to seem unrewarding and unattractive. In that cultural vacuum, the Buddhist ideal of enlightenment began to take its place in the minds of upwardly mobile Chinese youths. Although many kinds of Buddhism would find their way into China, at the time when Buddhism first arrived Mahayana Buddhism was a relatively new and exciting development in India and Central Asia. That excitement and a sense of superiority would catch hold in China. Within a few centuries Mahayana would come to dominate Chinese Buddhism and maintain that position throughout its history.

Buddhism was, of course, not without detractors in China. From the very beginning criticism of Buddhism as a foreign tradition, unsuitable to Chinese culture, would be frequently leveled. The practice of celibacy by monks and nuns seemed to ignore the long-standing Confucian demand for filial piety and the continuation of family lines through marriage and childbirth. Buddhist practices of cremation violated native Chinese burial customs and concepts of the soul that had emerged many centuries earlier. Monks and nuns, following the apolitical developments of Indian Buddhism, refused the Chinese custom of bowing to the emperor, setting off an enormous controversy. And the Indian custom of monastic begging just seemed to run against the grain of local Chinese sensibilities. These criticisms and others were initially potent, but over time Chinese Buddhists were either sufficiently persuasive or sufficiently flexible to revise Buddhist practice into forms that were acceptable on Chinese terms.

The first Buddhist sutras and meditation manuals began to be translated into Chinese in the second century CE. From that point on this literature grew rapidly and was disseminated broadly. Buddhist missionaries from Central Asia and then from India arrived in the centuries that followed to take up teaching positions and to translate important texts into Chinese. In the fourth century an order of Buddhist nuns was established, opening up the possibility of engagement in religious activity for women as well as professional career possibilities that were previously unavailable to women. By the fourth and fifth centuries the impact of Buddhism was being felt among all Chinese social classes, including aristocrats and government officials. Government-sponsored temple construction and large-scale translation projects would have the historical effect of committing Chinese society to long-term Buddhist influence. Although Confucianism and Daoism continued to exert strong intellectual and social influence, Buddhism had entered the intellectual life of China in so prominent a manner that at least from the fifth through the ninth centuries it would command pride of place.

During the Tang dynasty (618–907), Buddhism would reach the apex of its cultural dominance in China. By that time, Buddhist monasteries had spread throughout the land and served as the first universities and intellectual centers of China, similar to the way that Christian monasteries functioned as the primary educational institutions of Europe, eventually evolving into universities as we know them today. In the wake of the economic and creative advances of the Tang era, Chinese Buddhism would engender new philosophical trends in Buddhism, new forms of religious practice, and religious art and institutions that would spread throughout East Asia.

Buddhism's central cultural position in China would not be maintained, however. In the middle of the ninth century, a Daoist-influenced emperor, reclaiming the old idea that Buddhism was a foreign tradition, would order and oversee the wholesale destruction of over four thousand Buddhist temples throughout China and force over a quarter-million monks and nuns to return to lay life and back onto tax rolls. Although Buddhist institutions would survive this devastating attack and rebuild, evolving in new and impressive directions, the high point of Chinese Buddhist influence had passed. By the fourteenth century, a revival of interest in Confucian ideas and texts had gained a powerful foothold. And when a version of the earlier civil service exam took Confucian literature as its basis, the necessity for upwardly mobile young men to focus on those texts rather than Buddhist ideas and practices assured the downward spiral of Buddhist influence in China. From the fourteenth century to the beginning of the twentieth, neo-Confucian intellectual developments would upstage Buddhism among the Chinese cultural elite, leaving Buddhism largely to farmers and working-class citizens whose access to the elite literary culture of Confucianism was limited. Buddhist temples and monasteries remained in operation everywhere throughout China, but after the fifteenth century Buddhism no longer held a leading position in the culture.

2.10. What are the most distinctive features of Buddhism in China, Vietnam, Korea, and Japan?

Expanding out from China, Buddhism established itself on the Korean peninsula in the fourth century and in Japan from the sixth century onward. Buddhist culture took hold quickly and decisively in both of these places and would have a profound impact on virtually every dimension of Korean and Japanese lives. Vietnam, like Tibet, was in the interesting position of receiving its Buddhism from both Indian and Chinese sources. Early hints of Buddhist ideas and practices entered Vietnam from India through Southeast Asia and continued to flow into Vietnam as other Southeast Asian cultures developed. But especially in Chinese-dominated North Vietnam, these early influences would be overwhelmed by constant cultural influence working its way south through China over many centuries.

Each of these Pacific Rim cultures would develop its own style of Buddhism, each gradually taking a shape that would inevitably seep into neighboring cultures. Overwhelmingly, though, China would be the engine of Buddhist creativity and development in East Asia, constantly sending waves of new Buddhist culture out from its center.

The Chinese canon of Buddhist texts constituted a major advancement for Buddhism as a whole and a legacy that may continue to play itself out over the next few centuries. Two factors are important here. First, because thousands of Buddhist texts made their way to China, and because those who received them had no means of sorting them in terms of importance or origin or date, they ended up translating virtually all of them and over time constructing formulas for classifying them according to their relative importance. Second, the invention of printing in China at the height of Buddhist textual production meant that mass printing would quickly disseminate these texts throughout East Asia and by that means guarantee their survival over the centuries.

No other culture in the world had this incredibly efficient means of producing written documents until centuries later, and its impact on Buddhism and virtually everything else cannot be overestimated. At first individual texts were produced and disseminated in this innovative manner. But then the idea arose that all Buddhist texts could be printed together in a government-sponsored official version. The first printed edition of Buddhist sacred texts—containing over a thousand different texts, some in multiple translations—was completed in 983, and many other printed editions and catalogs of them would follow over the centuries. Today the greatest of these is the modern Japanese edition of the *Taisho Tripitaka*, published in fifty-five massive volumes produced between 1924 and 1932. Over these many centuries, the Chinese invention of printing would give a particular shape to East Asian Buddhism as well as constitute a vital contribution to the entire history of Buddhism.

One inevitably important characteristic of East Asian Buddhism is the sense of world affirmation that can be seen in indigenous traditions like Confucianism and Daoism. Because rebirth, the idea of repeated cycles of human life, was not native to China and competed with other ways of understanding death, belief in reincarnation never took hold to the extent that it had in India. Although it excited the Chinese imagination and continues to play a significant role in the way Buddhists imagine their lives, not all Buddhists in this part of the world find it either compelling or necessary. One reason for that reluctance was the widespread sense in China that the desire to get out of the cycles of life was misguided and that it cast the life we have in an unnecessarily negative light. This acceptance of—indeed, fascination with—the cyclical nature of all life was celebrated in many indigenous forms of Chinese thought, most notably perhaps in Daoism but also in Confucianism. Mature Chinese Buddhism would inevitably absorb this native sense of life affirmation, scaling back some of the otherworldly temptations that occasionally arose in India through its focus on the ubiquity of human suffering.

One of the easiest places to see the merger of incoming Indian Buddhist ideas with indigenous Chinese ideas is in the use early Buddhists made of Daoist concepts and sensibilities. Early translators of Buddhist texts into Chinese had no choice but to locate within the Chinese language concepts that were parallel to the Buddhist concepts that they wished to communicate, and this reservoir of indigenous concepts tended to be Daoist. Important symbols such as the Dao itself found their way into the center of Buddhist translations, and that meant that Chinese readers would inevitably understand Buddhism in Daoist-flavored terms.

Even when Chinese translators were aware of the extent to which this "matching of meanings," as they called it, misrepresented the original text, they had no serious alternatives. "Misrepresentation" really meant "re-presentation" of an idea in somewhat altered form. Buddhism was undergoing change, just as the Buddhist concept of impermanence had claimed. These alterations formed what Chinese interpreters came to consider new and improved versions. By the Tang dynasty, schools of Buddhist thought and practice were being produced in China that had no precedent in India or Central Asia. Tientai, Huayan, Chan, and Pure Land Buddhism are the most famous and successful of these Chinese Buddhist inventions.

2.11. How did Buddhism take hold in Tibet and Mongolia, and how did these cultures develop their own unique Buddhist style?

Given Tibet's geographic proximity to the home of Buddhism in northern India, it would be natural to assume that the transfer of this religion to Tibet would have occurred quite early in the history of Buddhism. But that is not the case. For centuries, as Buddhist travelers passed back and forth along the Silk Road, they passed through Tibetan-controlled lands, encountering Tibetans sometimes as disinterested bystanders and sometimes as bandits seeking wealth from the richly endowed caravans. Yet during this segment of early history there is no evidence of Tibetan interest in Buddhism. In the seventh century CE, however, as greater and greater impact from Central Asia, China, and India began to be felt, and as the political and military consolidation of Tibet began to take hold, Buddhism became a serious cultural influence in Tibet.

As is true everywhere else in Asian Buddhist cultures, Tibetan Buddhism would absorb and accommodate much from indigenous cultural sources, in this case from the native Bon tradition steeped in animistic interpretations of the natural environment, along with the practices of magic, divination, and exorcism. Tibet's astonishing geography and climate would also have a substantial bearing on the resulting cultural synthesis. Tibet's status as "the roof of the world" is almost literally true: much of the land stands more than ten thousand feet above sea level. Its forbidding mountain ranges, high-desert landscapes, and blistering wind and snow storms had shielded Tibet from most travel and commerce and had set the stage for Tibetans to experience and understand life's austerity, precariousness, and beauty.

In what is often referred to as the first wave of Buddhist incursion into Tibet in the seventh and eighth centuries, the sources of Buddhist influence were geographically diverse, from Central Asia and China as much as or more than directly from India. Often these different forms of Buddhism were competitive and occasionally hostile to one another. This diversity is symbolized by the famous monastic debate before a Tibetan king as judge. The Indian Buddhists, led by the renowned monk Kamalasila, argued that enlightenment was attained through a slow, gradual process of development, while the Chinese representative ridiculed gradual development in favor of nonconceptual experience and the sudden breakthrough of awakening.

The Tibetan king's decision in favor of gradual enlightenment had both political and cultural ramifications. Politically it allowed him to distance Tibet from the threat of Chinese incursion, and culturally it favored literacy and learning, crucial for a still preliterate Tibetan culture. Moreover, it helped give Tibetan Buddhism its particular orientation, which is comprehensive, or catholic in the sense of being universal. Tibetan Buddhists felt an obligation to incorporate and reconcile all previous Buddhist thought and practice, which has meant that, rather than culturally focused or oriented to a particular kind of person, it developed in a way that offers something spiritually relevant for everyone.

In this first wave of Buddhist influence, a Tibetan system of monastic training began to develop. Supported both politically and financially by the monarchy, Tibetan monasteries established an educational program for boys and young men that would remain intact all the way into the modern era. Although this system of monasteries ensured the stability of Tibetan culture, the political structure that supported it was highly unstable, and by the ninth century monastic Buddhism was being persecuted.

Following this period of cultural and political fragmentation, a second wave of Buddhist influence began in the tenth century. Buddhism recovered under royal patronage, and the Buddhist links to India began to bear substantial fruit for Tibetan culture. Different monastic orders or lineages of Buddhism took shape, always in debate with one another, a condition that led to greater and greater sophistication in their teachings and practices. Different monastic orders, known by the color of their hats (either red, black, or yellow), have vied with one another throughout the history of Tibetan Buddhism, but their differences are less doctrinal than they are lineage-related. Having placed great emphasis on the role of the *lama*, a guru or teacher, in the transmission of both Buddhism and Buddhist enlightenment, monastic orders were differentiated primarily along these genealogical lines.

The canon of Buddhist texts that were gradually and painstakingly translated into Tibetan language from many Buddhist languages (but especially Sanskrit) is one of the monumental contributions that Tibetans have made to global Buddhist culture. Divided into two major segments, the *Kanjur* contains the Buddhist sutras and the *Tenjur* consists of documents of many other kinds, from Buddhist scholastic treatises to texts on ritual, medicine, and astrology. This canon includes many Buddhist texts long lost to other cultures and constitutes the basis of Tibetan monastic learning.

Although literacy and learning were the hallmarks of Tibetan monastic culture, another, less rational and more experiential orientation within Buddhism drew greater influence from the Shamanic culture of early Tibet. Because the kind of Buddhism that was migrating to Tibet from India was the newly emerging Tantric orientation—with its use of divinities, rituals, visualizations, and mantras—these two contrasting forms of Buddhism could be synthesized within monastic culture. The sophisticated mental cultivation of monastic meditation could be combined with the ecstatic visions and altered states of consciousness of the native shamans into one comprehensive form of Buddhism that is uniquely Tibetan.

Mongolian Buddhism began in the fourth and fifth centuries CE through contacts with Central Asian and Chinese culture via trade and exploration. Little is currently known about its development prior to the rise to power of the Mongols under the notorious Genghis Khan (1162–1227). Uniting all of the nomadic tribal groups along the steppes of northeast Asia, the Mongols invaded and conquered most of Eurasia, from the Caucasus all the way through China. This unlikely political expansion allowed various forms of Buddhism to be imported into Mongolia. Based on cultural and geographical similarities, Tibetan Buddhists were awarded pride of place in the Mongol court, soon converting the Mongolian ruling class and thus most Mongolian Buddhists to the Tantric style developed in Tibet. Solid links between these two Buddhist cultures have been maintained virtually since the thirteenth century. In fact, the lineage of Dalai Lamas derives from this link between the two when in the sixteenth century Altan Khan awarded the prestigious title of Dalai, or "Great Ocean," Lama to one of the Tibetan monastic orders. Indeed, the fourth Dalai Lama was an ethnic Mongolian.

Mongolian Buddhist development was often linked to developments in China. The Qing dynasty (1662–1911), originating in Manchuria, to the immediate northeast of China, drew heavily upon Mongolian and Tibetan Tantric Buddhism in order to differentiate itself from the mainstream of Chinese Buddhism without needing to abandon Buddhism altogether in governing this enormous and highly diverse population. As a result, Mongolian Buddhism has had a huge impact on the shape that Chinese Buddhism has taken over the past half-millennium. Tantric Buddhism continues to be practiced in Mongolia today as the world comes to learn more and more about this previously remote and little-known culture.

2.12. What is Tantric Buddhism, and how has it developed as a unique form of Buddhism?

Tantric Buddhism can be understood as the final stage of development of Indian Buddhism, beginning in the fifth and sixth centuries of the Common Era and continuing until the eventual demise of Buddhism in India centuries later. Indeed, another name for this form of Buddhism is Vajrayana (Vehicle of the Thunderbolt, or Diamond), which places it in line as a third developmental stage after the "small" and "great" vehicles, or *yanas* (Hinayana and Mahayana). But two qualifying considerations are important here. The first is that Tantric religious themes were not unique to Buddhism; they were shared among all Indian religions during this period. The second is that Tantric Buddhism was primarily a further development in Buddhist practice rather than thought, in that this tradition maintained the philosophical orientation of Mahayana Buddhism along with its principal texts. Sharing a final goal of complete Buddhahood on behalf of all living beings with Mahayana Buddhism, Tantric Buddhists claimed that their practice was a faster, more skillful method to attain that goal.

Some of the most distinctive Tantric practices can be traced back to the *mahasiddhas*, wandering ascetics or yogis who lived on the fringes of Indian society in funerary grounds, forests, and caves, thus rejecting the comforts of established society. These religious aspirants sought magical powers, or *siddhis*, such as levitation and paranormal vision, and the folklore about them was so vivid and noteworthy that it was almost inevitably absorbed into Buddhist and other established religious cultures. Stories about these wandering yogis circulated widely throughout India for a few centuries as they were being gradually absorbed into more established traditions of religion.

Tantric Buddhism produced a substantial corpus of texts over a period of four or five centuries, beginning as early as the sixth or seventh century CE. These texts, called *Tantras*, are presented as secret teachings passed down directly from the

Buddha himself through special lineages of powerful yogis. *Tantras* have traditionally been classified into four groups or stages of practice culminating in what is called *supreme yoga*. At all stages, however, they maintain that authentic practice requires receiving the teaching from a sanctified teacher, a guru or lama.

Earlier Buddhist themes that are developed in the *Tantras* include the following:

1. The unity of the profane world of *samsara*, the ordinary world we experience throughout our lives, and *nirvana*, reality as experienced by the Buddha.
2. The theme of the seed or embryo of Buddhahood that can be found within all human beings.
3. The idea that this innate inner enlightenment is the power behind and the source of all spiritual practice.
4. That elements of the profane world that are otherwise shunned can be employed in religious practice to accelerate the experience of awakening, including sexuality, profane language, ritual engagement, and the breaking of taboos.

The ascendancy of Tantric Buddhism in India coincided with later stages of the absorption of Buddhism into Chinese culture, and as a consequence its influence on Chinese, Korean, and Japanese Buddhism is unmistakable. But as a distinct form of Buddhism it would always exist on the margins of East Asian culture. Tibet and Mongolia, however, would take up the traditions of Tantric India and develop them further over many subsequent centuries.

2.13. What is Zen Buddhism?

Zen is an East Asian form of Buddhism that has attained a global following in the contemporary world. Originating in China during the Tang dynasty (618–907), Zen spread to Vietnam, Korea, and Japan to become a dominant form of Mahayana Buddhism in each of those countries. The word *zen* is the Japanese pronunciation of the Chinese *chan*, which was an early transliteration of the Sanskrit Buddhist word *dhyana*, meaning "meditative absorption, deep awareness, and equanimity." As this meditative tradition of Buddhism came to prominence during the late Tang and Sung dynasties, legends circulated about the powerful and unusual character of awakened Zen masters. Once written, these stories became one of the great literary traditions of East Asian Buddhism.

Although meditation had always been an option for Chinese Buddhists, most Buddhists focused their practice on sutra study and learning or on ritual and devotional practices of various kinds. The earliest Zen masters were meditation teachers, sometimes located in rural retreat settings. They taught a variety of techniques for meditation, often beginning with mindfulness of breathing but culminating in forms of concentration in which thoughts and sensations would be allowed to pass through the mind as quickly as they entered, without grasping or attachment. Intense focus on these contemplative practices led Zen teachers to de-emphasize Buddhist knowledge and learning in favor of a direct realization of awakening. They focused on seated meditation (Japanese *zazen*) as a means of experiencing the *Buddha nature*, or enlightenment potential, within all people and understood this experience as a sudden breakthrough to the true nature of oneself and all things.

The legendary founder of Zen is Bodhidharma, a Persian meditation master from India famous for his outspoken irreverence and his deep meditative absorption. Legends maintain that Bodhidharma offended the emperor of China by denying that his financial support of Buddhism had earned him great karmic merit, and that Bodhidharma then retreated from society to spend nine years meditating while facing a cave wall without moving. A Bodhidharma slogan became the hallmark of Zen: "A special transmission outside of the sutras without dependence on language; direct pointing to the mind, seeing one's own true nature, and becoming Buddhas." Later Zen Buddhists maintained that Zen awakening (Japanese *satori* or *kensho*) was handed down from one master to another from the Buddha himself to Bodhidharma and beyond through a process of mind-to-mind transmission without reference to doctrines or sacred texts. One formative story claims that one day when the Buddha was teaching a difficult concept, no one seemed to understand. Then, when asked a question about the point of practice, the Buddha gave his answer nonverbally by holding up a flower. Everyone was baffled by this response, except Mahakasyapa, who in that moment received transmission of enlightenment directly from the mind of the Buddha.

These legends, products of later Zen imagination, were just the beginning of a tradition of stories about eccentric Zen masters that dominated East Asian culture for centuries. These stories became so central to Zen practice and identity that they virtually replaced the Buddhist sutras as the focal point of spiritual attention, becoming over time a voluminous literary tradition. This "transmission of the lamp" literature took a variety of forms over the centuries but came to be organized as a genealogical chart of the history of mind-to-mind transmission, stories about the accomplishments and antics of one Zen master followed by each generation of enlightened disciples. Central to these stories were accounts of what transpired when one Zen master encountered another or when students of Zen posed questions to their teacher. These "encounter dialogue" stories more than anything else served to build the reputation of Zen masters as powerful embodiments of Buddhist awakening. What makes them exceptional in Buddhist literature is the extent to which they feature Zen awakening coming to expression in daily life—in work, in conversation, and in everything else, from communal meals to travel, as a form of monastic practice.

Even though one of the strict rules of early Buddhist monasticism was that monks and nuns were not to engage in work of any kind so that they could devote themselves entirely to meditative practice, Zen traditions rejected this rule. Initially this legitimization of work may have been out of necessity, the need for early rural monasteries to support themselves without government patronage. But soon thereafter spiritual justification followed: if Zen awareness doesn't fundamentally transform the quality of actual lived experience in the world, what's the point? All Zen monks and nuns—even Zen masters—were by monastic rule expected to participate in the work life of the monastery. Stories describing awakened speech or actions set in these work environments are often featured in Zen literature.

Although the doctrinal teachings of Buddhism were clearly de-emphasized in Zen, the most significant of these teachings emerge in nondoctrinal form throughout Zen teaching and literature. For example, an important Mahayana concept, the seed of Buddhahood, was deeply influential in the origins of Zen. But even though this formal concept never appears in any Zen text, Zen masters each have their own ways of persuading students to visualize Zen awakening as an eruption of what is already within them rather than as an acquisition of something they previously lacked. Since Zen awakening is thus a realization of what is already there deep within, any aspect of life— an ironic comment, humor in the workplace, seeing something extraordinary—was thought to be capable of evoking this experience.

Zen masters throughout East Asia were known for their participation in the arts, especially poetry, painting, and calligraphy. Building on Chinese Daoist traditions, a Zen aesthetic featured natural settings, simplicity rather than refined sophistication, muted tones of black and gray on white rice paper in painting and calligraphy, sparse but potent phrases in poetry, and images of hermits dwelling in the natural world as their primary subjects. As in Zen awakening, inspiration in the arts would be sudden and intuitive, with strong connections to ordinary earthly life.

Traces of the early Zen tradition appear in Vietnam almost as early as they do in China, in the sixth to eighth centuries. These Vietnamese versions of Zen thrived over the subsequent centuries through regular contact with Zen in southern China. Zen (or Seon) was transmitted to Korea as the Chinese tradition developed in the eighth and ninth centuries, and in the twelfth century these Zen traditions were transmitted to Japan. The Zen best known in the West comes most directly from Japan. In all of these locations, however, Zen thrived as an elite form of Buddhism for many centuries.

2.14. Why did Buddhism disappear from India after being disseminated virtually everywhere else in Asia?

This is one of the great ironies of Buddhism. Having spread virtually everywhere to become the dominant religion in Asia, Buddhism would cease being a major tradition in India, where the Buddha himself had been born and taught. There is no simple story to be told here; the demise of Buddhism in India occurred slowly and perhaps somewhat imperceptibly over half a millennium. By the end of the thirteenth century, Buddhism had been virtually eliminated from South Asia, with the exception of Sri Lanka.

Among the most important factors in this transformation were changes in the economic structures that had financed the rise of Buddhist institutions. Dependence on the private support of individual households and, later, wealthy families was not a reliable means of sustenance in medieval India. No doubt the rise of the Brahman caste and the substantial influence that this religious aristocracy had on socioeconomic structures was also a strong counterweight to continued Buddhist dominance.

The natural and easy flow of influences between Buddhism and Hinduism was another factor. Because Buddhism was held in such high regard, other religious groups borrowed its successful ideas and practices. Shaivism and Advaita Vedanta—two prominent forms that native Hindu traditions had assumed—borrowed a great deal from Buddhism, and many of their most successful ideas flowed back the other direction, into Buddhism. As a consequence, it became increasingly difficult for most people to tell the difference between them. One could imagine an Indian village family finding these religious traditions virtually indistinguishable, so that less and less seemed to be at stake in deciding which one they might adopt and patronize.

Invading armies were another major factor in the decline and eventual disappearance of Buddhism from India. First were Hun invaders from central Asia. Although they did not settle in India permanently, while occupying Buddhist territories the invaders targeted Buddhist monasteries and temples for destruction. Many of these Buddhist complexes fell into ruin and closure in the sixth, seventh, and eighth centuries. If that weren't enough—and it almost was—Turkish invaders began to arrive in the eleventh century with beliefs and practices that conflicted strongly with Buddhist and Hindu traditions.

Muslim prohibitions on visual representations of religious subjects meant that they were inclined to destroy much of the monumental architecture in northern India. In addition to the elimination of Buddhist images, these invasions plundered the remaining wealth that had sustained Buddhist monasticism. By the end of the thirteenth century, Buddhism existed in India only as fragments of a lost world.

2.15. How has Buddhism been shaped by contact with the West?

Beginning early in the nineteenth century, Buddhist cultures in Asia were confronted by the forceful challenges of Western imperialism and colonization. Colonizing powers proclaimed the superiority of their own traditions, primarily Christian monotheism, modern science, and democratic government. They denounced ritual practices, traditional Asian cosmologies, reincarnation, monasticism, polytheism, and the unfamiliar morality they encountered upon arrival in Asia. In response, some Buddhists simply took the pragmatic course of de-emphasizing their own Buddhist roots and adopting modern Western influences—sometimes Christianity but more often capitalism and secular humanism. Others, however, came to the defense of Buddhism by reinterpreting their traditions in light of these new influences. This latter response has produced what we now call "Buddhist modernism." Many of the forms of Buddhism that have become prominent in the West are in fact these modernized forms of Buddhism that evolved in response to the challenge of confrontation with the West.

Although there are many distinct versions of Buddhist modernism, they share several characteristics and tendencies. They tend to accentuate the rationality of Buddhism and understand the basic teachings of Buddhism to be in accord with modern science. They reduce or ignore the theistic and supernatural elements that evolved throughout Buddhist history, while downplaying the roles of ritual, monastic leadership, and reincarnation. Meditation practices are given pride of place in Buddhist modernism, while other practices have been de-emphasized. Because substantial grounds for all of these interpretations of Buddhism can be found in the early sutras and throughout the tradition, Buddhist modernism can be understood to have revived the essence of the Buddhist tradition. On these grounds, modernists proclaimed the superiority of Buddhism to other world religions and by the middle of the twentieth century began to win converts around the world.

Here is a quick overview of how these developments unfolded. Early European and American colonists were not in Asia to appreciate the traditions they found; their assignment was to take control and to promulgate the power and superiority of Western culture. Naturally, therefore, the early administrators, soldiers, and missionaries wrote home with disdain for virtually everything they found abroad, and no one in the West had any reason to doubt their accounts. By the middle of the nineteenth century, however, European scholars

began to take an interest in these new languages and the ancient traditions they represented. Their work gradually began
to represent Buddhism in a new and more positive light.

A significant turning point was the 1879 publication of a
best-selling book by Sir Edwin Arnold, *The Light of Asia*, which
told the story of the life of the Buddha in glowing romantic
terms while suggesting strong parallels to the best aspects of
Christianity. Under the influence of this book and others following it, a World Parliament of Religions was held in Chicago
in 1893. Although attention at this event was overwhelmingly
paid to the highly educated, native English-speaking Hindu
Swami Vivekananda, two Buddhists were also recipients of
great praise: Anagarika Dharmapala of Sri Lanka and Soyen
Shaku from Japan. From this point on, praise of Buddhism in
the West has tended to overshadow criticism.

Then, through the middle of the twentieth century,
culminating in the 1960s, the writings of D. T. Suzuki, an educated modern lay Zen interpreter, had an enormous impact
on the reputation of Buddhism in the West, and this development led to the creation of new, modern versions of Buddhism
in both Asia and the West. Suzuki presented Zen Buddhism
to English-language readers as compatible with the best
in Western philosophy and science while at the same time
representing a radical alternative to those modern Western
traditions. Zen emphasized direct, intuitive experience as
opposed to linear reasoning, offering an unfiltered percep-
tion of reality. Suzuki emphasized Zen's inner connection to
global mysticism, European romanticism, and the American
Transcendentalism of Emerson and Thoreau. This new international version of Zen Buddhism attracted enormous attention in the West and began to influence the way Zen was
conceived in Japan.

At virtually the same time in India, where Buddhism had
not been a significant presence for almost a millennium, a
new Buddhist movement grew quickly to assume a prominent political and cultural role. Founded by B. R. Ambedkar

in the 1950s, a neo-Buddhist movement called Navayana Buddhism converted hundreds of thousands of impoverished Hindus among the "untouchable" outcastes of the Indian caste system. Since Buddhism had rejected the caste system, claiming that all human beings are equal in spiritual capacity, Buddhism seemed to open opportunities to the lowest classes of Indian society. Navayana rejects some traditional Buddhist ideas and practices—monastic renunciation, karma and re-birth, for example—in order to bring Buddhism into alignment with the struggle for social, political, and economic equality. The quest for political and social reform represents one of the earliest versions of what has since become known as "Engaged Buddhism." Modernized forms of Buddhism continue to de-velop and thrive today. (We will return to these issues in the final chapter, on contemporary Buddhism.)

2.16. How did Western Buddhism emerge, and how is it related to Asian Buddhism?

Buddhism in the West has grown rapidly since the middle of the nineteenth century, along two quite different streams. The first of these is the Buddhism that accompanied immigrants to the US and then later to the UK, Europe, Australia, New Zealand, and elsewhere. The first substantial influx of Buddhist immigrants were Chinese laborers who arrived in California in the 1850s and 1860s to work in the gold-mining industry, on the transcontinental railroad, and then on subsequent rail connections. Although several early Buddhist temples were constructed, for the most part laborers moved from job to job without settling long enough in one area to justify building a temple. But priests and others trained to engage in Buddhist rites and services were in demand in these communities, and the few people sufficiently knowledgeable about these traditions would have served in this capacity.

Japanese immigrants, mostly farmers initially, arrived shortly thereafter, using Hawaii as a transition point long before it became an American territory or state. Although a small number of immigrant Buddhists from Southeast Asia and Korea arrived in the first half of the twentieth century, the vast majority arrived after the Korean War and the war in Vietnam. In each case, however, wherever a substantial gathering of immigrant Buddhists settled, temples have been constructed and Buddhist priests have been imported to serve the religious needs of these communities. Each of these forms of Buddhism remains as different from one another in the West as they had been in Asia.

Immigrant Buddhist communities of this kind were motivated to practice and to maintain their Buddhist traditions with great care for their authenticity. One can imagine the satisfaction that would have come from participating in this one important source of native identity to hold families together in a new cultural world that would have seemed both fundamentally different and for a long time relentlessly hostile. Preserving the integrity of these ancient traditions has therefore been a high priority. Nevertheless, it would be a mistake to think that immigrant Buddhists in the West have felt no motivation for change. The very different cultural environment in which they found themselves gave rise to new ideas about the role and character of Buddhism. On occasion, interest in melding with or accommodating Western styles of religion has produced very basic change—putting Christian-style pews in Buddhist temples and giving central importance to the sermon in religious services, for example. Finally, the fact that second-, third-, and fourth-generation Asian immigrants would have had such different experiences from those of their earliest immigrant ancestors has given Buddhist temples in the West reason to modernize and change as a way to appeal to very different generations of Asian American Buddhists.

The second channel through which a distinct Western Buddhism has emerged is more homegrown. In the nineteenth and twentieth centuries, scholars at Western universities labored to translate sutras and other basic texts from Buddhist languages, as well as to provide description and analysis of Buddhism, enabling non-Asians to gain access to this foreign tradition. This early surge of interest in understanding Buddhism as one of the great religions and philosophies of the world led eventually to the founding in the 1960s of Buddhist studies as a substantial academic discipline now practiced in virtually every college and university in the West. This scholarly reproduction of Buddhism in English and other European languages has provided the basis upon which others have taken a more committed and practice-oriented interest in Buddhism.

All of this and considerably more has given rise to a Buddhist culture of converts in the West—Americans, Europeans, and others who, born into Christian, Jewish, or secular families, have nonetheless come to consider themselves Buddhists. We have already seen that a well-established pattern throughout the proliferation of Buddhism in Asia has been that Buddhism is reinterpreted and subtly reshaped on each occasion that it enters a new language and culture. That pattern clearly holds true in the West. As carefully as American Zen Buddhists might strive to replicate the authentic Zen of Japan, for example, changes in the character of Buddhism are inevitable.

Foremost among the kinds of Buddhism that have so far inspired conversion are insight meditation traditions from Southeast Asia, Tibetan Buddhism, and Zen Buddhism. Insight meditation, primarily learned from Thai and Burmese teachers, is now widely available throughout the West in a lay or nonmonastic form. Early pioneers of these meditation practices—Sharon Salzberg, Jack Kornfield, and Joseph Goldstein—have taught thousands of Americans and Europeans the basic techniques of mindfulness and insight meditation at well-established centers such as those in Barre, Massachusetts, and Spirit Rock, California and elsewhere.

Tibetan Buddhism began to attract attention beginning in the early 1970s, especially after the Dalai Lama became internationally known and admired. In the 1950s and 1960s, as many other Tibetan lamas were exiled from Tibet, they began emigrating to the West and establishing Tibetan Buddhist institutions in the UK, then in the US, Europe, and beyond. Among the most prominent and influential of these were Geshe Wangyal, Tarthang Tulku Rinpoche, and Chogyam Trungpa Rinpoche. Two enormous aids in their efforts to promulgate Tibetan Buddhism were the publishing houses Shambhala and Snow Lion. The first fully accredited Buddhist college in Western Buddhism, Naropa University in Colorado, helped develop and disseminate the modernized Tibetan teachings of Chogyam Trungpa Rinpoche.

Zen Buddhism attracted initial attention in the West through the voluminous writings of D. T. Suzuki, which in turn gave rise to a brief literary and artistic movement with Jack Kerouac's publication of *The Dharma Bums* and *On the Road* and Gary Snyder's Japanese- and Zen-inspired poetry. Slightly later, Robert Persig's *Zen and the Art of Motorcycle Maintenance* put the word *Zen* into wide circulation. Shortly thereafter, however, these romantic Zen influences gave rise to rigorous Zen meditation practice. Although there is much history to this larger story, the most significant event in Western Zen would no doubt be the founding of the San Francisco Zen Center by the Soto Zen master Shunryu Suzuki in 1961, with subsequent expansions to the Zen Mountain Center in Tassajara, south of San Francisco, and the Green Gulch Zen Center, north of the city. From these three historic beginnings, Suzuki-inspired Soto Zen practice has been disseminated to many American and European Zen centers.

Each of these traditional forms of Asian Buddhism that have settled in the West has evolved in its new setting, and this process is no doubt still in the early stages. In every case, new ideas, new practices, and new ways of being a Buddhist gradually emerge to add to the enormous Buddhist heritage that began in India two and a half millennia ago.

3

BUDDHIST TEACHINGS

3.1. Do Buddhists believe in God?

As you may have noticed, our discussions so far have hardly mentioned God. Buddhist teachings aren't oriented around a theistic concept of God, God as creator or ruler or savior. Although images of the Buddha as savior or supreme being have at various times and places had a significant impact on Buddhism, the early texts demonstrate that the Buddha himself was instead focused on the dharma, teachings aimed at helping human beings step out of their self-imposed suffering by cultivating enlightened or awakened ways of living their lives.

The point of being a Buddhist was health: mental, physical, and spiritual well-being at the highest level. Throughout the Buddhist tradition, the dharma was referred to as the medicine and the Buddha as the physician who had formulated the most effective methods of diagnosis and cure. Although practitioners would have to administer the cure themselves, the dharma would provide prescriptive guidance.

This diagnosis sought to explain and to rectify the most fundamental human problem: the ubiquity of *dukkha*, most often translated into English as "suffering." In one early sutra, the Buddha claims that he teaches about only two things: suffering and the cessation of suffering. In what is traditionally taken to be the very first sutra, suffering and its alleviation are the focus throughout. Buddhism's primary concern is clear.

The manner in which the teachings focus on suffering is also eminently practical. They aspire to present an effective way to remedy the deep-seated pain in human existence and to create in its place an awakened life of wisdom and compassion. In a famous parable, the Buddha asked what we would think of someone just hit with a poisonous arrow who insisted on asking long-winded theoretical questions about the archer, the bow, and the arrow, while the poison seeped slowly into his bloodstream. Absurd, of course, in the same way that all speculative discussions not directly aimed at repairing the overwhelming suffering in life are absurdly beside the point.

For these reasons it is more appropriate to think of the dharma as a system of training in life rather than as a belief system. Although there are certainly many beliefs or ideas that Buddhists would regard as important, there are no lists of required beliefs. Beliefs provide direction and orientation toward practice, while practice is a concrete way to transform one's life. Training in Buddhism comes in a variety of forms, as we will see in the chapter on Buddhist practices, but these cover the wide spectrum of insight or discernment, ethics or virtue, and concentration or meditation. All of these areas of training require thoughtfulness, however, and the Buddha was well-known to have insisted that each person think for himself or herself. "Don't take my word for any of this" is a paraphrase of the Buddha's teaching in the *Kamala* sutra. "Instead look deeply into the matter for yourself and decide on your own."

3.2. What are the Four Noble Truths?

The Four Noble Truths are frequently presented as the central teaching of Buddhism, ideas around which everything else in the teachings can be organized. Although this hasn't always been true, it is a good place to begin.

The Four Noble Truths aren't "truths" in the sense of a creedal or propositional doctrine. Rather, they take the fundamental problem of human life, the problem of suffering, and provide both an analysis of the problem and a solution. The truth about suffering, the cause of suffering, a way to envision the end of suffering, and a path of practice aimed at alleviating suffering and achieving an optimal state of human existence called nirvana. These truths are "noble" in two senses: they are the way of life of those people who are thought to be truly noble in character, and serious meditation on these four will ennoble the thoughtful practitioner.

The Four Noble Truths begin with the basic reality of suffering. In addition to the suffering felt in physical pain, we suffer in disappointment, loss, anguish, fear, loneliness, stress, worry, hatred, bitterness, resentment, alienation, and on and on. Regardless of how happy we might currently feel, we know that we are never far from the next emotional downturn. The overall focus of Buddhist teachings is on our mental health, and the first step toward health is to acknowledge and understand our own personal experience of suffering. Suffering is a simple, fundamental fact of life that healthy individuals have learned to face directly and effectively.

The second truth concerns the causes and conditions that give rise to our suffering. Although these differ from person to person and must be understood by each of us individually, Buddhists claim that there is one overarching, general cause that is worth our careful attention. A deep-seated thirst or craving (*tanha*) is at the root of all suffering. This thirst leads to grasping or attachment, a desperate holding on as though our lives are at stake. But, Buddhists claim, this thirst is ultimately unquenchable. Although we may satisfy a powerful craving by obtaining the object of desire, we all know how temporary that satisfaction will be. It will be followed almost immediately by another, perhaps equally strong desire, and then by another without end. The basic principle is that true happiness can never be obtained by possessing the objects of our desire. Unfulfilled desires and unrelenting attachment bring human suffering in the form of resentment, depression, anger, hatred, and deep frustration. We thirst for life to fulfill our wishes, and this unfulfilled craving underlies all of our moods. But that relation to our desires is based on a tragic misconception: the unrealistic hope that when the object of our craving is in our possession we will finally be happy.

The third truth turns from analysis of the problem to the possibility of a solution: if you eliminate or ameliorate the conditions that give rise to suffering, you will have eliminated or diminished that suffering. The primary point here is that the causes of suffering are located within you and are therefore within your power to change. You don't have to change the world so that it conforms to your wishes. What is required is a transformation of your own orientation toward the world. And, ironically, this inner change alters your relations to others, a position from which you might actually change the world. Craving and attachment can be replaced by other relations to the world that are deemed healthy by Buddhists, and healthy individuals tend to help create healthy communities.

The fourth and final truth lays out a positive path of change, known as the Eightfold Path, which names particular areas of human self-cultivation that enable an enlightened relation to the world. These healthy qualities of character are grouped into three categories: wisdom, virtue, and meditation. They call upon us to acquire an appropriate understanding and intention (wisdom); appropriate speech, actions, and occupation (virtue); and appropriate self-discipline, mindfulness, and concentration (meditation).

Although the Four Noble Truths are logically sequential, one following the other, the Eightfold Path does not specify a step-by-step sequence of practical engagement. Serious Buddhist practitioners dwell on as many of them as possible in whatever order makes practical sense in individual circumstances. But in the end, all of these dimensions of human life require thoughtful, disciplined transformation in order to approach the state of mind and character that Buddhists regard as "awakened" from the cycles of suffering.

3.3. Does the emphasis on human suffering make Buddhism pessimistic?

It is clearly true that Buddhism focuses its attention on the issue of human suffering more directly and more intentionally than any other major world religion. And if you juxtapose that central theme to the joy of salvation in some other religions you might be tempted to conclude that Buddhism is more pessimistic in overall character, or that it underplays or even denies the joy and pleasure in human life. This characterization, however, misses several important points.

First, if you are willing to face the truth about human life, you will see that most people are not particularly happy. We suffer not just occasionally but frequently in anxiety, loss, fear, exclusion, disappointment, and more. Buddhists would claim that they are simply willing to bite that bullet of truth and not delude themselves. The theme of suffering in Buddhism is simply their diagnosis of the most basic human problem. Not to begin by admitting the difficulty of our situation is simply foolish, they claim.

Second, coming to terms with suffering in life is the starting point for doing something about it. From this perspective, denying the reality of suffering and pretending otherwise renders us incapable of addressing the problem. Recall that the truths announced in the Buddha's first sutra are both suffering and the cessation of suffering. The latter point is a message of hope, a declaration that a life that is free of suffering is available to all. Buddhists take this to be the good news that the Buddha's awakening made possible. Buddhists claim we can do something about the problem of suffering and begin living a life of peace, experiencing the joy of open, compassionate relations to others and the world.

Buddhists place emphasis on individual responsibility and self-reliance, but those themes are tempered by generous offers of assistance and guidance. The attitudes of fatalism and resignation that have sometimes been attributed to Buddhism have no basis in the fundamental teachings.

3.4. What other teachings about the causes of suffering are important in Buddhism?

The Four Truths name craving, thirst, or attachment (*tanha*) as the cause of human suffering. Another teaching, called the Three Poisons, provides more nuance to the Buddhist understanding of this basic human problem. Three particular states of mind, it is claimed, poison our lives and produce profound levels of suffering. These are greed, hatred, and delusion. The first two are opposites: in mental states of greed, we pull things toward ourselves, and in hatred we vehemently push them away. Buddhists consider both of these to be caused by intense craving, a thirst to obtain what we want and a corresponding thirst to avoid what we don't want. Pushing and pulling our way through life, we never find the satisfaction that our efforts seem to promise.

The third poison is delusion or ignorance. If we misunderstand the way the world is and if we misunderstand who we are, we will continually make decisions and act in ways that are not at all in the interest of living a healthy, enlightened life. There is a sense in which delusion is an even more fundamental cause of suffering than craving, in that delusion gives rise to craving. Because we misunderstand the world and our place in it, we long for things that will not satisfy us. The Buddha claimed that living the way we do is based on a deluded grasp of our nature and situation in the world.

3.5. What are the delusions that Buddhists regard as detrimental to life?

A central Buddhist teaching called the Three Characteristics outlines three important aspects of life that we typically misunderstand. The three characteristics of reality are *impermanence, suffering,* and *no-self,* and to these we add a fourth principle called *depended arising* for purposes of clarification. The Buddha's enlightenment experience is often referred to as a moment in which he came to know and see things as they really are. These four features of reality provide a glimpse of this Buddhist way of knowing and seeing.

Impermanence is a universal truth for Buddhists: that everything in our world changes, without exception. Everything is always in flux, even if its movement is slow and the thing in question appears to be very stable, like the ground under our feet. Failure to recognize the extent and pervasiveness of change is regarded as the most common delusion of human life. The second characteristic of existence is that suffering is not an accidental or occasional aspect of our lives but deep and universal. Realizing this fact and working with it is, for Buddhists, the only way to begin to live a mentally and spiritually healthy life.

Third, and somewhat counterintuitively, Buddhists maintain that there is no permanent self, no unchanging, unaffected part of you that constitutes the real you down beneath all of the changing aspects of your life. This teaching is often translated into English as "no soul." This basic misunderstanding of who or what we are is thought to lead to further suffering. The Buddha declared that everyone lives in this delusion until they discipline themselves in the cure of meditative self-understanding.

Fourth—our additional factor—is dependent arising, a teaching that helps clarify the other three. Things are impermanent, but not randomly; their change is orderly and sometimes predictable. Dependent arising means that everything becomes what it is and changes the way it does based on particular causes and conditions. In the absence of those causes and conditions, the thing in question can't become what it is. The Buddhist teachings on dependent arising, impermanence, and no-self cohere with the teachings about human suffering and its alleviation to form the inner structure of Buddhist culture and practice. We address these four teachings in more detail now.

3.6. How do Buddhists understand the impermanence of all things?

From a Buddhist point of view, the first feature of existence that human beings must understand and adapt to is the impermanence of all things. Everything is fundamentally transitory. Nothing will remain what it is right now. All things come into existence at some point in time, change over the course of their existence, and then finally pass out of existence. Impermanence, therefore, encompasses both the change occurring to all things in the world and the fact that they will one day die and disappear. Perhaps most significant for Buddhists is the recognition that change is the fundamental nature of human mental and emotional life. Like everything else in the world, our mental life is always on the move. Thoughts replace one another in rapid succession, as do perceptions, moods, feelings, motives, and every other aspect of our inner lives. Nothing stays put for long, and human beings are no exception to that rule.

Although the basic truth of that realization is important to Buddhists, most important is how that insight helps people understand the patterns of suffering in their lives. Whatever might be giving us great pleasure at the moment will soon cease to do so. Momentary feelings of assurance and well-being will pass away, sometimes turning into their opposites. Similarly, whatever currently causes us pain and emotional anxiety will alter its hold on us, shifting into another state that may be just as unpredictable. Love will be lost, gained, or just fade away; riches will come and go, as will disappointment, fear, and everything else we might experience. One of the central teachings of Buddhism is that reacting to the reality of impermanence by trying to hold things still or to keep things the way they have been is a tragic human mistake. We live in a mental world of uncertainty and instability, and if we are unable to understand and to accommodate that basic fact, additional suffering will follow. Craving for stability and certainty in the face of change and the threat of suffering, we are sure to be disappointed and are likely creating the conditions for even more suffering.

3.7. What does dependent arising *mean, and what role does it play in Buddhist thought and practice?*

One crucial idea that appears prominently throughout the history of Buddhism in all cultures is a concept translated as "dependent arising" or "dependent origination" or sometimes "dependent co-arising." So important is this idea that an early sutra has the Buddha announce, "One who sees dependent arising sees the Dharma itself." The earliest understanding of this idea is expressed in the phrase "When that arises, this comes into being; from the cessation of that, this too ceases." This means that all things come into being, pass through their various states over time, and then disappear due to the effects of the necessary causes and conditions. When the exact conditions necessary to support the existence of something come into being, then the thing will arise. As those conditions change or disappear, the thing in question will also change or disappear. And this causal influence runs in all directions. Interdependence is the character of all things; nothing is what it is on its own.

The earliest uses of this idea were specifically aligned with the intentions of the Four Noble Truths, which explain how suffering arises, how it takes the particular forms that it does, and how it might possibly be alleviated. Again, we see that the practical, ethical concern for the way we live our lives is primary. These teachings are among the most psychologically insightful in Buddhism. They provide helpful explanations for why people do what they do, how it is that they have the particular fears or resentments or other aspects of character that they do. The teachings lay the groundwork for analyzing what our harmful, self-destructive, and habitual mental states are and how to create the conditions in which they will cease to have a hold on us. Buddhist meditation exercises focused on dependent arising were specifically designed to foster this change.

A specific version of this overall formula that was very influential early in the history of Buddhism and continued to be consequential in Theravada traditions of Buddhism is called the Twelve Links of Conditionality, or the Wheel of Becoming. Beginning with the arising of ignorance, a sequential pattern of twelve steps was developed to show how the appearance of one thing inevitably leads to another and another and another, ending in the despair and misery of a life that is enveloped in suffering and that has failed to actualize its potential to awaken from this destructive pattern. The links can be broken at any point along the chain, but doing so requires adopting practices that condition other, healthier ways of living.

Philosophically the teachings on dependent arising helped develop the Buddhist view of constantly changing lives in an impermanent world. They give shape to an understanding of *how* things change and help persuade practitioners that they have the capacity and the tools to change their ways of living. The worldview that these teachings illuminate is of a dynamic, fluid universe in which all parts are intertwined and interdependent. Everything is seen to be in process, whether rapidly or slowly, and everything is what it is depending on what else is having an influence on it.

Buddhists came to refer to this understanding as another aspect of the Middle Way. The Buddha had rejected his own ascetic practices of self-torture in declaring Buddhism to be a middle path between self-indulgence and extreme self-denial. This same language of the "middle" was then used to show how the Buddhist teachings of dependent arising plot a middle course between the view that everything exists permanently in isolation from other things (eternalism) and the view that ultimately nothing truly exists at all (annihilationism). Dependent arising articulates *how* things exist: all things exist through their causal and conditioning relations to other things, and as a consequence everything changes along with any change in these relations. All of these ideas apply as much to human beings as to any other thing in the world, and this is the primary reason Buddhists claim that there is no eternal self or soul.

3.8. What does the Buddhist teaching of no-soul or no-self mean?

Anatman, the idea that human life is not organized around a permanent, divine inner essence—a soul—is perhaps the signature doctrine of Buddhism, the concept that most recognizably sets Buddhism apart from other religions. The contrast with other successful religious and philosophical systems in India at the time could not have been greater. The foremost teachers of that era taught a variety of ways to conceive and experience the ultimate aim of an authentic religious quest, the discovery of the True Self within.

The Buddha rejected that common idea. There is no eternal soul, no inner, permanent *you*, he argued. Not only is the external world impermanent and always in flux, but so is every aspect of the inner life of human beings. And not only do all entities in the outer world arise dependent on factors beyond themselves, but so do all aspects of human life—mental, physical, and spiritual. Nothing about human beings is any more permanent and independent than anything else in the world.

The Buddha encouraged meditation on this thought. Look deeply within, he instructed. Is there anything you can experience there that appears to be unmoved, permanent, unrelated to, and uninfluenced by anything else? His own answer was a firm no. What you do find, he claimed, is a complex movement of physical and mental phenomena that are dependent on each other and on other conditions out in the world. We experience many complicated aspects of ourselves, but from a Buddhist point of view none among them stands apart from the always impermanent world of dependent arising.

To illustrate one dimension of this idea, an early and famous sutra describes the meeting of a Buddhist monk with an incredulous Greek king, Milinda. The king finds this Buddhist idea of no-self absurd, so to explain it the monk points to his royal chariot and asks whether the axle is the chariot, or the wheel perhaps. None of them, it turns out, is the chariot itself. Yet if you remove the parts, there is no chariot. *Chariot* therefore is just a convenient way to name the temporary coming together of these particular parts, just as *self* is a convenient way to name all the converging aspects of a temporary human life. But neither *chariot* nor *self* names anything independent and timeless.

Some doubtful teachers accused the Buddha of nihilism. Doesn't this mean that human life is really nothing at all, they objected? Not so, responded the Buddha. Nihilism is an extreme error avoided not by leaping to the mistaken idea at the other extreme but by a Middle Path between them. That all aspects of human being are temporary and dependent on forces beyond themselves splits the difference between eternalism, the view that human beings are permanent and divine, and nihilism, the view that in the end nothing truly exists. We neither exist permanently nor don't exist at all.

Moreover, Buddhists think that dwelling on the idea of a human soul, or "deep self," can have troubling personal and ethical implications. They regard the idea of the soul as a delusion fostered by fearful grasping or misguided attachment. Related to this grasping is attachment to possessions, the deep desire to accumulate and to protect our "selves" with riches. The very concept of an independent, eternal self is thought to encourage further egoism and isolation from others. Meditating on the no-self idea, Buddhists seek a kind of personal character that is not undermined by fear and insecurity and that exudes lovingkindness and selfless compassion. Insight into one's own selflessness was considered to be a crucial dimension of nirvana. Experiencing the way things really are in the absence of this eternal soul was thought to give rise to a way of living that was naturally at ease, unselfish, and instinctually open to others—the very definition of a fully actualized life for Buddhists.

But don't become riveted on any negative doctrine, the early Buddhist texts stress. In fact, in some dialogues the Buddha is reported to have rejected the ideas of both self and no-self. For experienced meditators, the very question of whether there is a soul or a lack of soul doesn't arise. For them, the no-self teaching was useful as a strategy of spiritual diagnosis and therapeutic healing but not worthy of becoming a new point of intellectual attachment.

3.9. If there is no self or no soul, what then am I? How do Buddhists understand being a person?

The Buddha's most important answer to this question was that there are five aggregates (*skandhas*) of human life, the Five Skandhas. Each aggregate or component is impermanent, always changing, and influenced both by other components and by the world beyond us, thus affirming the Buddhist idea of no permanent, independent self. These five elements of human life are given substantial elaboration and explanation. First, we are aware of bodily experience, including perceptual experience of ourselves and the world around us through five senses: vision, hearing, smell, taste, and touch. Second, we respond to perceptions with a variety of feelings: pleasant or unpleasant, attractive or repulsive, and so on. Third, we classify and conceptualize our experience through a variety of concepts and thought processes. Fourth, all of this motivates us to act: it gives rise to will or volition, including basic desires. Finally, all of these components are linked together in human experience to form a particular self-awareness. We are conscious of ourselves as individual persons with bodies, feelings, thoughts, and motivations.

English translations of these five aggregates, or *skandhas*, differ significantly. But the important realization is that there is no permanent and independent self behind these ever-changing components. It's not that I *have* a body, feelings, thoughts, a will, and self-consciousness. It is rather that I *am* this set of factors as they interact with each other and the world in continual transformation. I am the current state of my body, feelings, thoughts, will, and self-consciousness as they take the particular shape they do in this moment.

Of course, Buddhists recognize the continuity of human experience, since memories and feelings and so on are linked together within an individual through dependent arising. Still, because we tend to inflate our own sense of stable identity, Buddhists emphasize the extent to which we are very different than we were a decade or a day or an hour ago. Our bodies differ, our thoughts, our moods, our aspirations, all aspects of our experience change. Everything about us has shifted in some significant way. This, they claim, is good news because it means that human beings are malleable and that we can have a role in shaping the transformations that will occur in our lives.

The Buddhist theory of the Five Skandhas suggests a different kind of self-understanding than most people have naturally. It gives practitioners a set of concepts to guide meditation on what is taking place within their minds and lives and a different way of understanding how we might alter the destructive tendencies that inevitably arise in our physical, mental, and emotional lives. It also challenges us to do this through serious introspection. If you consider yourself an immortal soul or self, try to find what that means. It asks us what in our experience of ourselves has led us to that way of thinking about ourselves. Can we locate and identify anything that meets the criteria of immortality—permanence and independence?

The Buddhist claim is that if we meditate on any aspect of our experience, we will find that everything is constantly changing, even from one moment to the next, and that no evidence can be found for what other early Indian religions had called the *atman*, the immortal deep self. Thus the Buddhist understanding on these matters maintains that a human being is a complex flow of physical, mental, and emotional events and that none of the components in this flow can legitimately be claimed to be the True Self, even if one thought that flows through my mind posits such a self to help calm life's fear and insecurity. A better strategy, according to Buddhists, is to acknowledge what we are in a way that accords with our actual experience and learn how to live skillfully with this acknowledgment. That realization of selflessness constitutes a significant dimension of the awakening that Buddhists seek.

3.10. How do Buddhists understand death and the possibility of an afterlife?

A famous early Buddhist story describes the Buddha responded to a situation of overwhelming grief over the reality of death. A mother's young son has died. Her grief is so intense that she approaches insanity in refusing to accept that the boy is dead. She is sent to the Buddha for help, and in response he gives her an assignment. She is to go through town door to door, inquiring of each family whether anyone living there has died. Having finished her inquiry through the entire village, she is to bring the Buddha a single mustard seed from all the homes that have escaped the ravages of death. At each house she hears the stories of how death occurred, how the family grieved, and how following this period of grief they were eventually able to move on in life, essentially receiving counseling from everyone who has also experienced the death of a loved one. After combing the village and failing to find even one mustard seed, the woman arranges for the cremation of her son and returns to the Buddha to offer her findings and gratitude. Understanding the wisdom of the Buddha's prescription, she becomes a Buddhist nun and soon achieves nirvana.

Death is universal and inevitable, and some form of grief at the death of others is appropriate and emotionally necessary. To accept the inevitability of death and to understand it so profoundly that you can move forward in life is the Buddha's prescription. This fits perfectly with the basic Buddhist teachings that all things are impermanent, that all things come into existence and pass out of existence dependent on numerous causal and conditioning factors, and that for human beings there is no permanent, independent soul that carries on past death. Dying is one link in the causal processes wherein all things pass over into other things, and then into other things, without end.

Meditation on death, especially on one's own upcoming death, is a well-developed practice in many forms of Buddhism. Failing to realize the preciousness of the opportunity to live, we squander our time in life. From the earliest eras of Buddhist practice, meditations were designed that would guide Buddhist practitioners toward taking life seriously, thereby helping them avoid the overwhelming regret or anxiety that often comes toward the end of a person's life. The illusion of immortality was regarded as the most brazen of the ego's various attempts to define itself as permanent and independent. Death meditations aspire to curtail these illusions and to cultivate the capacity to face life and death with balanced equanimity rather than fear.

The particular ways that death is understood and the practices that accompany death in Buddhist societies vary from one culture and one historical epoch to another. Local customs of practice and understanding were already in place when Buddhism arrived. It stands to reason, then, that these customs continued to have some influence on understanding in each culture even after Buddhism came to be the dominant religion.

In the early Indian history of Buddhism, we find a sophisticated understanding that did have an influence everywhere Buddhism traveled. And this understanding shows very clearly that the Buddha too was deeply influenced by the culture into which he was born. Beliefs about human reincarnation were already on their way to acceptance throughout India when Buddhism came into existence. The Buddha's response appears to have been to accept this dominant idea but to revise it to match the immense transformation in worldview that Buddhism represented. To understand how, we will need to discuss two of Buddhism's most characteristic and controversial ideas: karma and rebirth.

3.11. What is the Buddhist understanding of karma?

Karma is not just a Buddhist idea. It's an early Indian idea that became so persuasive that virtually all religious traditions in

India adopted some form of it. And it's not an exaggeration to say that karma is now a global idea, one that has some degree of influence in almost every culture. Karma is the central moral principle for Buddhists. It explains how it is that our own actions influence our future. It holds people accountable for what they do and assumes some degree of freedom for all human beings to make choices and to alter their life experience over time. Karma stipulates that every act gives rise to an appropriate consequence. This consequence follows directly from the act itself without supernatural intervention. A good or bad act produces naturally good or bad outcomes that are not rewards or punishments dictated by divine beings. Karma functions like dependent arising but is restricted to the human sphere.

Early Buddhist texts judged the qualities of human actions in terms of their being healthy or wholesome, unhealthy or unwholesome for human lives. A healthy or wholesome act is one that adds to the integrity and balance of the actor's body and mind. It moves the person incrementally closer to the ultimate condition of nirvana. Unhealthy or unwholesome acts have correspondingly negative effects. They obstruct or slow a person's movement toward a healthy, enlightened existence. In other words, you become what you do. In Buddhism, the effect of karma is restricted to intentional acts. Unintentional acts are regarded as karmically neutral. What we choose to do and knowingly do has a strong effect on our lives. A person's state of mind and intention determine the quality of the act and therefore the quality of the karmic consequences of that act. Good karma doesn't necessarily follow from adherence to rules, precepts, or commandments but is instead an expression of motivations for actions that are nonclinging, unselfish, wise, and compassionate whether or not they are in adherence to the rules.

Unwholesome, unhealthy acts are thought to be motivated by the Three Poisons, also called the Three Roots of Evil. Greed, hatred, and delusion poison the mind by providing unenlightened motivations. Actions motivated by greedy clinging, by hateful aversion, or by misunderstanding or denying the truth give rise to karmic effects that degrade the mind and character of the actor. Conversely, wholesome acts are motivated by generosity and openness to others, by friendliness, tolerance, and compassion as well as by insight and profound understanding. Such acts give rise to positive karma that shapes the life of the actor. Karma is the principle in Buddhism that guarantees this dimension of ultimate accountability. Positive and negative karma resulting from healthy and unhealthy choices throughout life determine not just how we end up in this life but how we are to be reborn in another life.

3.12. How is karma related to the Buddhist idea of rebirth or reincarnation, and how is this afterlife thought to work?

Buddhists reason that a person's karma extends throughout his or her life and then beyond, into another life that has been shaped by the particular qualities of that person's karma. The specific character of the new life—gender, personality, physical attributes, social standing of the family, literally everything—is dependent upon the character of the previous life. So the reborn life is different from the previous life, which was itself shaped by the one before it, and on and on going back an unlimited number of generations. There is no beginning to the cycles of birth, death, and rebirth.

In English it has become the custom to distinguish between *rebirth*, which applies to Buddhism, and *reincarnation*, which is the Hindu or Brahmanical way of understanding death and afterlife. In various forms of Hinduism, a person's soul—sometimes referred to as *atman*—is reincarnated in a new life and body. But Buddhists had already denied that human lives are grounded in an eternal soul. Lacking an enduring core, then, who or what is reborn in the Buddhist understanding? The official Buddhist answer is nothing: there is no such permanent core within human lives or anything else.

But there is, many Buddhists believe, a causal connection between the character of one life and a previous life from which it has been reborn. The relation between one life and the next is not reincarnation or transmigration of the same soul into another body, but a causal connection between two lives without reference to any substantial, immortal core. In the same way that for Buddhists no substantial core remains even within one life—just patterns of interacting bodily states, thoughts, emotions, and so on—there is no substantial core that transmigrates from one life into another. Death is just another event in ongoing dependent arising, the existence of everything giving rise to something beyond itself.

Of course, not all Buddhists have understood death and rebirth in the same way. So although traditional Buddhists have seldom been inclined to deny the reality of rebirth since the idea appears frequently in the Buddhist sutras, what they make of this teaching often differs substantially from one culture to another or one person to the next.

To envision the scope of these differences, imagine a range of concepts of rebirth running along a spectrum. At one end of the spectrum some Buddhists, when asked, will say that at death they, or their soul, will be reborn in a new life. Given this understanding, they will make every effort to live a virtuous life so that good karma will make their next incarnation better than this one. It is not difficult to see, however, that this way of talking about rebirth contradicts the basic Buddhist teachings of no soul, impermanence, and dependent arising. But not all Buddhists understand or care about such abstract teachings; they are much more concerned about their own welfare in a future life. Their understanding amounts to belief in reincarnation of the soul quite like other religious traditions in India, even though the Buddha's critique of that view can be found throughout the sutras.

A person located at the middle of the spectrum might say, following the words of the Buddha, that a reborn individual is neither the same as nor different from the one who came before. A famous analogy attributed to the Buddha puts it this way: The relation between one life and a subsequent life is like the relation between one burning candle passing its flame on to another candle. The first candle causes the second to light, but we're unable to say whether the two candle flames are the same or different. *Neither* was the Buddha's answer. The relation between one life and the next is one of cause and effect. This option preserves the no-soul idea and a sense of individual life after death. If there is an orthodox view on this matter, a rendering like this would be it. But not all Buddhists accept this version of rebirth either.

Finally, at the other end of the spectrum is the idea that rebirth is more accurately conceived collectively rather than individually. Looking at it this way, the karma of individuals is ultimately the karma of families, of communities, of nations, and of humanity as they interconnect. The karmic decisions and acts of one generation set the stage upon which the subsequent generations play out their own decisions. Rebirth, to the extent that this word is still appropriate, is understood collectively as whole generations receiving karmic influence from past generations. The karma of all past acts is inherited by the new generation, shaping their lives, their choices, and their possibilities. Everything has its influence and is reborn into everything else, over and over. From this perspective, the effects of our lives continue on forever, but this way of framing that continuity seeks to avoid the egocentric fallacy of clinging to the self by recognizing how all things eventually disperse into other things.

No doubt many other versions of rebirth can be found along this continuum of views, not to mention the rejection of the whole idea of rebirth among some modern Buddhists, especially those who were not originally raised in an Asian Buddhist context in which the idea of rebirth seems quite natural and obvious. No test of orthodoxy forces any Buddhist to adopt a particular position on the issue of afterlife, or any other idea, for that matter. Claims for the absolute status of any

doctrine are seen to partake of the kinds of clinging and attachment that Buddhists strive to overcome.

The exact mechanics of rebirth also differ to a considerable
extent from one Buddhist culture to another. Some Buddhists
understand rebirth as occurring almost immediately after
death, while others, most notably Tibetan Buddhists, understand rebirth as happening after an interim state between
death and rebirth. Some Buddhists believe that consciousness
is the aspect of a human life that continues into the next life,
even though few people experience any connection between
their current life and the one before it. Others claim that there
is no one dimension of a human life to transmigrate into another, just a continuum of causal forces shaped by the acts in
previous lives. But for many Asian Buddhists, the idea that
human lives are recycled in some way is as natural and obvious to them as the idea in Western cultures that people do
not go through such cycles.

3.13. What role do karma and rebirth play in Buddhist moral culture?

Karma and rebirth play basically the same role in Buddhist
moral culture that God's commandments, judgment, and
heavenly rewards play in Christian cultures. They provide
good reasons to care about the quality of one's own behavior
and good reasons to discipline oneself to remain in accord with
the moral standards of one's society. The teachings of karma
and rebirth communicate the idea that it matters what you do,
how you treat other people, and what kind of life you live.
These teachings encourage Buddhists to prefer and to seek out
"wholesome" acts, as they are called in Buddhism, acts that are
not poisoned by greed, hatred, and delusion.

The karma accrued from such wholesome choices and acts
is thought to improve the quality of one's life, but also and
perhaps more important, the quality of one's rebirth, no matter
how you conceive of that life as yours. The Buddhist emphasis

is on state of mind, on motivation, and on developing the freedom to choose a healthy, wholesome life rather than to be compelled into unhealthy choices by out-of-control craving. Those who manage to live wholesomely will have arranged the future life that they deserve. Those who fail to live such a life know that they are responsible and will suffer whatever consequences follow from their failure.

The moral system of karma and rebirth in Buddhism allows for greater nuance in outcomes than an either/or system of heaven or hell. Everyone gets exactly what they deserve. The benefits and privileges of a future life are thought to emerge in exact proportion to the moral quality of a previous life. And although failure produces serious bouts of suffering in the next life, everyone gets another chance to get it right. This system of morality is so compelling that many Buddhists focus their religious lives on the accumulation of positive merit rather than directly on the ultimate goal of Buddhism, nirvana. They focus more attention on setting themselves up for a better future life in which they will be capable of striving for awakening to nirvana than they do on attaining that ultimate goal now.

Samsara is the Buddhist name for these cycles of birth, death, and rebirth. To focus one's attention on a better rebirth is, by virtue of that self-centered orientation, to remain within the cyclical world of samsara and to put off for the future the serious quest to put an end to these cycles in the attainment of the ultimate state of nirvana. Although some Buddhists express disappointment about this accommodation to a somewhat self-centered and diminished goal, the reigning attitude is more often that everyone will eventually recognize that nirvana is the only goal really worth pursuing, and until they do recognize that, at least they are striving to live a better, healthier life within the cycles of samsara. The teachings of karma and rebirth have been the backbone of Buddhist moral culture for over two millennia now, and although they have undergone regular reinterpretation and adjustment over the centuries, they still exert a strong influence on the lives of millions of Buddhists.

3.14. What is the Buddhist view of the larger cosmos?

Buddhist thought and practice are primarily focused on human awareness and self-cultivation, not cosmology. Its most pressing questions concerned how to live an awakened human life, what such a life would be like, and what practices would most effectively get you there. These human concerns require a larger setting, however, a cosmology or view of the full universe that would place the human quest for awakening in context. For the most part, in this area of concern, Buddhists accepted the picture of the overarching world that developed in northern India at the time Buddhism was founded.

The contrast of this cosmology with Western religious worldviews is startling. Rather than human history being the focus of all creation, the Indian worldview that Buddhism inherited was unlimited in time and space and diversely populated. It included a number of beings in the universe in addition to animals and people: the gods, goddesses, and other beings described in early Indian mythology. Although the Buddha was reluctant to claim that the universe is eternal, the time frame for the world was immense, far beyond human understanding. For all conceivable human purposes, the universe was thought to have no beginning and no end. Spatially, Buddhist cosmology was also expansive, the realm of our planet being just one small system in a vast universe of diverse worlds. Buddhists had no conception of creation, and no all-powerful deity whose creative act brought everything into being.

The Buddhist universe was neither static nor prearranged. The ideas of impermanence and interdependence implied a worldview of continual change and great complexity, including processes of expansion and contraction that were thought to be cyclical over enormous periods of time. The cosmos was divided into three realms: the sensual realm, the realm of form, and the formless realm. Located within these three realms were six possible destinies: the destiny of hell, the destiny of hungry ghosts, the destiny of all kinds of animals, human destinies, the destiny of spirits or deities called *devas*, and the destiny of *Brahmas* or gods in the realms of form and formlessness. Karma from a past existence determined which destiny a being would come to inhabit, with the destiny of hungry ghosts and animals being the result of negative karma from habitually unwholesome acts. All of this was considered to fall within the scope of samsara. Nirvana wasn't a place or a realm but a state beyond all time and space. Further divisions and categories in this cosmology proliferated as Buddhist history moved forward, but this initial conception is vast enough to get a full sense of the scope of Indian imagination within which Buddhism operated.

Another distinct and interesting feature of Buddhist cosmology is the diversity of interpretations that it allowed. From the very beginning it is clear that this cosmological picture could be understood both as a depiction of the outer world and as a map of one's inner, psychological world, with lines of connection drawn carefully between them. Beings inhabiting the cosmos in the various realms were correlated with particular states of mind and emotion. The range of possible human experience was mapped upon the possible realms of existence into which someone might be reborn. The concrete detail of this mental map matched the detail of the universe as a whole. Emphasis on one side or the other—outer or inner world—was considered a matter of personal choice.

Although the cosmology described here had an influence on all Buddhist cultures, as Buddhism expanded in history and geography so did the range of cosmological reflections and the input coming from non-Indian cultural contexts. This is one area of Buddhism that has been impermanent and open to changing vision, and so far at least Buddhist adaptation to the worldview of contemporary science has been seamless.

3.15. Does faith play a role in Buddhism? And if so, what?

The simple answer to this question is, yes, of course, faith is entailed in the practice of Buddhism. But it is important to stipulate what specific understanding of faith Buddhists might have in mind. Although the Pali and Sanskrit words that typically get translated as "faith" do appear in classic Buddhist texts, no one would argue that they are among the best known or most frequently emphasized concepts. Still, the role they play is crucial. The first and most important meaning of *faith* in Buddhist texts is a sense of commitment or dedication to the practice of the teachings. This kind of faith is required to motivate initial and ongoing practice. If you lack confidence that the study or practice of Buddhism will be beneficial in some way, then you are unlikely to bother. Buddhists recognized early on that faith is a necessary component of practice in the sense that the capacity to take risks and to work at the teachings in a disciplined way requires a faith-like dedication.

Later Buddhists emphasized the realization that the very first step as a Buddhist is the most important one. They called this "the thought of enlightenment," or the "aspiration for enlightenment." Those who lack the thought that enlightenment is a serious possibility, those without any image in their mind of what an awakened life might be like, lack the motivation, the rationale, and the power to move ahead. You don't strive for anything unless you have a strong sense that it is worth pursuing. The formation of that thought of enlightenment is what provides the faith to initiate the discipline of pursuit.

There is one very common practice among Buddhist monks and nuns that shows this kind of trust and commitment most clearly. The Three Jewels are recited by all monastic Buddhists every day from the first day of their initiation to their death. They chant, "I take refuge in the Buddha, the dharma, and the sangha," that is, they commit themselves and their lives to the founder of Buddhism, to the teachings of Buddhism, and to the order of monks and nuns whose support and encouragement are so important. This is clearly a confession of faith, an act of meditation that is meant to empower their practice and sustain that drive in spite of all difficulty.

One reason that many modern Buddhists have been reluctant to use the word *faith* in connection with their practice of Buddhism is the legacy of an opposition between faith and reason that has burdened Western Christianity. Faith in this sense is blind and refuses the enormous benefits of critical thinking. In that sense, faith is the act of forcing yourself to believe a doctrine or teaching that reason and evidence would eschew. This sense of faith and this way to have faith is, for the most part, at odds with the way Buddhism has been structured.

For Buddhists, reason is vital. You can't possibly understand the teachings and be empowered to practice them without substantial thinking. Among several early sutras that stress this point, the most famous is the *Kalama* sutra. In it the Buddha argues against taking his word for the truth of the teachings without engaging in your own internal critical investigation. Without personal testing and verification, without direct awareness of the validity of the teachings, no commitment can legitimately be made. Much nuance and certain qualifications are added to this picture of faith in later Buddhist developments: the Lotus sutra, the Pure Land sutras, and in a few of the greatest of Japanese Buddhist theologians. We will address these developments shortly.

3.16. What further teachings distinguish Mahayana Buddhism from earlier traditions of Buddhism?

Diversity of approach to Buddhism is almost as old as Buddhism itself. Regional differences, differences of language, economic systems, class, prior religious heritages, all had a bearing on how the dharma would be understood. But beginning possibly as early as the first century BCE differences in approach among Buddhists would crystallize into the most basic division within Buddhism. Criticisms leveled by some monks on earlier ways to understand and practice Buddhism gave rise to a movement called Mahayana Buddhism, set in contrast to Theravada or Hinayana Buddhism. The teachings of Mahayana Buddhism evolved through the first several centuries of the Common Era in India and elsewhere as Buddhism spread into entirely new areas in Central and East Asia. Here are the primary Mahayana innovations, several of which will be described in greater detail over the next few questions.

First, newly composed Mahayana sutras were open to the latest literary developments in India, expanding into new genres, languages, and methods of teaching. In contrast to the earlier sutras, Mahayana texts were expansive and imaginative and described a universe of immense proportions and depth. The worldview of Buddhism underwent a significant expansion in terms of cosmology and the scope of human activity. Second, at some point Mahayana teachings began to extoll a new vision of the Buddhist path, referring to it as the "bodhisattva path." Bodhisattvas are Buddhist saints who vow to continue through countless cycles of rebirth until all sentient beings have been saved from suffering. This "vow of compassion" suggested a criticism of the earlier Buddhist quest for awakening as betraying the ideal of selflessness. Enlightenment, they claimed, is the birthright of all beings, and no one should accept it until everyone can be fully liberated from suffering.

Third, these teachings led to the name Mahayana, the "great or large vehicle." Buddhism had already been pictured as a vehicle, a means of transport from samsara, this ordinary life of suffering, to nirvana. The Mahayana was imagined as great or large because, rather than emphasizing individual or personal awakening, it aims for the enlightenment of all living beings collectively. Everyone was invited to ride the great vehicle to nirvana. By contrast, pejorative language referred to earlier Buddhists as Hinayana, a small vehicle capable of transport for individuals but not for whole communities.

Fourth, although the image of the Buddha had already been evolving through the first few centuries of Buddhist history, Mahayana Buddhists absorbed the influence of theistic religions across Eurasia to allow conceptions of the Buddha as a compassionate savior deity. Fifth, Mahayana extended the meaning of the earlier Buddhist concepts of impermanence, dependent arising, and no-self to form their central philosophical idea, emptiness (*sunyata*), which helped develop the teachings of the interdependence of all elements in the universe.

Sixth, pushing the meaning of emptiness a step further, Mahayana activists claimed that one of the Buddha's primary teachings extolled the necessity of skillful means (*upaya*) or methods of communicating the Buddhist dharma. Being skillful enough and profound enough in the Buddhist teachings enabled flexibility in relation to the rules of the sangha. The rules of the *Vinaya* were not discarded but made relative to appropriate contexts. Seventh, all of these teachings transpired to reduce the importance of the distinction between monastic Buddhists and lay Buddhists. Men and women, working people, householders, and others were all in principle given equal status—anyone in almost any walk of life might undertake Buddhist discipline to attain full awakening. And eighth, based on these developments, a new concept of the inner Buddha nature within all living beings arose. Everyone has within them the seeds of Buddhahood, and these seeds can begin to germinate and unfold at any time.

These new extensions of teaching began to alter what it meant to be a Buddhist in Mahayana-dominant regions, and these developments are still evolving in Central Asia, Tibet, Mongolia, China, Korea, Japan, and Vietnam, as well as in pockets all over the world.

3.17. What is the Mahayana bodhisattva ideal, and how does it differ from the image of the Buddhist saint in earlier Theravada Buddhist traditions?

Although the word *bodhisattva* (literally "awakening being") appears in a variety of uses in early Buddhist writings, the most prominent of these is in reference to the Buddha himself prior to his full enlightenment experience. Its meaning is roughly "someone dedicated to striving for enlightenment—and getting close." Mahayana Buddhists selected this name for all seriously aspiring Buddhists and set this ideal in contrast to lesser aspirations. As this ideal evolved it entailed practitioners taking the "bodhisattva vow," a personal vow, either formal or informal, to seek enlightenment not just for oneself but on behalf of everyone equally and simultaneously. This ideal was implicitly and explicitly contrasted to the Theravada arhat, who, although compassionate toward the suffering of others, understands the path to awakening as an individual endeavor.

The bodhisattva path includes a few essential features. First, a person must hear the dharma spoken in a way that plants a seed of aspiration and discipline in the mind. This seed is thought to mature until it finally becomes *bodhicitta*—the awakening mind or thought of enlightenment—an understanding of what is possible to achieve and a deep commitment to strive relentlessly until that goal is attained. At this point practitioners take the bodhisattva vow, declaring internally and publicly that bringing enlightenment to all living beings is their ultimate goal in life, thus committing themselves to pursue a level of selflessness that would make it quite natural to strive toward the highest goal in life as much for others as for themselves.

The bodhisattva vow commits one to the practice of the Six Perfections, six dimensions of human character thought to have been perfected by the Buddha through his enlightenment experience. These are (1) the perfection of giving or generosity, the discipline of gradually learning openness to others; (2) the perfection of morality, the discipline of learning restraint from hindering others; (3) the perfection of tolerance or patience, the discipline of learning to be calm, balanced, and forgiving from a position of strength; (4) the perfection of energy and striving, learning to build the discipline, endurance, and strength to engage in enlightening tasks; (5) the perfection of meditation and concentration, learning inner contemplative skills that are essential to further refinements of consciousness and character; and (6) the perfection of wisdom, an embodied sense of the impermanence, interdependence, and selflessness of all aspects of reality, including oneself. While all six are to be practiced simultaneously, the first five can be perfected only when the sixth, wisdom, puts them into perspective. This means that one's generosity, for example, will fully come to fruition only when one's actions are pervaded by a deep awareness that support for others is just as important as support for you. Until then all striving for generosity will be partial, always limited by the lack of depth in one's self-understanding.

Practicing the Six Perfections, the bodhisattva deepens in wisdom and compassion, discovering at an advanced level that these two virtues are actually the same. Attaining wisdom about what all living beings really are gives rise to a natural compassion and the capacity to treat them as you would treat yourself. Moreover, Mahayana teachings stress that samsara and nirvana are nondual, which is to say that the enlightened commit to perfecting this world because there is nowhere else to go. Nirvana is not another world in another realm; it is the reality right before our eyes seen comprehensively and wisely.

Finally, the bodhisattva path was laid out in stages of accomplishment, in some cases related to the sequence of perfections. In fact, at some point a theory of ten stages for the bodhisattva gave rise to the addition of four more perfections. These stages move the practitioner from an awkward, disciplined effort at the outset toward a more natural, spontaneous desire for enlightenment, from a sense of being in personal training to one of being supported and empowered by the surrounding world. Although variations on the bodhisattva stages are common, they provide a sense that progression along the path can be measured to some extent and understood.

3.18. What is the Mahayana Buddhist teaching of emptiness, and how is it related to the bodhisattva's quest for wisdom and compassion?

Mahayana philosophy gives central focus to one concept, typically translated into English as "emptiness" (*sunyata*). Although this idea appears in early Buddhist sutras, it didn't become the subject of serious development until the first few centuries CE, when the *Perfection of Wisdom* sutras made it the central theme of the life of the bodhisattva. Emptiness was proclaimed the supreme therapy, the cure to heal all forms of greed, hatred, and delusion. The deepest wisdom was thought to be available to the bodhisattva in the experience of emptiness.

As a concept, emptiness came to be defined in terms of three fundamental Buddhist ideas: impermanence, dependent arising, and no-self. All things are empty. Of what? Of their "own being" (*svabhava*), their own essential "self," because all things change and all things depend on other things as causes and conditions for their own existence. If something did possess its own being, it would be permanent; it would never change. And it would be fully independent of everything else.

Mahayana Buddhist sutras argue that this is what the Buddha really meant by "no-self." Some commentaries on the teachings of the Buddha claim that although there is no permanent self, the elements that compose the self possess their own being in such a way that they can be experienced and analyzed in meditation. And this is what Mahayana sutras take great pains to deny in order to avoid what they see as philosophical attachment, a dogmatic holding onto something static. Nothing possesses its own power of being; everything comes into being and changes through time, dependent on the force of other things. That's what it meant to say that particular things are empty (*sunya*).

Occasionally Mahayana Buddhists were accused of nihilism, of *literal* emptiness. In reply they explained that emptiness doesn't entail the annihilation of anything. Everything exists as it was before—that is, in relation to other things and in process of change. Emptiness doesn't deny the existence of anything in our world; what it does is explain *how* it is that things exist. They exist through their connections to other things. This nondualism was the Mahayanists' way of subtly rejecting Indian monism, the view that everything is One, the same, identical. The Mahayana view is that things are not the same. They are different, except insofar as they are all empty, which means that they are related to each other, that they influence and shape each other such that when one thing changes, other things must change as well.

The intricate teachings on emptiness gave rise almost immediately to new ways of understanding the sangha and Buddhist society. Although it might be more difficult to awaken to the true nature of things—emptiness—if you were not a monk or a nun focused exclusively on that quest, nothing seemed to forbid lay people from becoming advanced bodhisattvas. And in a change of even greater proportions, nothing would require that Buddhists not be fully engaged in the ordinary social world. The seclusion of monastics began to seem unnecessary to some, since the purity of the monastery and the impurity of urban life were seen to be nondual; neither had a permanent essence that would forbid Buddhist participation. On these bases, one sutra imagined a wealthy lay person named Vimalakirti to be the most enlightened of all, even though he was involved in politics, businesses, even frequenting cabarets and gambling venues. If nothing has a fixed essence or static nature, anything and anyone can be transformed and liberated from the poisons of greed, hatred, and delusion.

3.19. How did the Buddhist understanding of the Buddha evolve?

Even though during his long life the Buddha resisted all tendencies to treat him as beyond human status, reverence for the Buddha clearly mounted with his reputation and with the success of the new religion. Nevertheless, the teachings held that the Buddha was a human teacher, one who had discovered a path to awakening from suffering in life. He was to be the object of great respect but not worship, and the common understanding was that when the Buddha entered parinirvana at death, he was no longer in or of this world. Legends grew after his death, however, and the practice of monks and nuns "taking refuge in the Buddha, the dharma, and the sangha" gradually gave rise to a conviction for some Buddhists that refuge in the Buddha would take the form of grace emanating from his universal compassion.

With the emergence of Mahayana Buddhism, earlier resistance to deification faded quickly, and new ways of understanding the Buddha developed. Rather than conceiving of the Buddha as far removed from the world, Buddhists began to have a religious sense of his continued active influence in their lives even after his death. Parallel to this development and no doubt influential on it was the appearance of sculptural images of the Buddha. Descriptions of religious experience in which someone had a vision of the Buddha began to spread in verbal and written form. Moreover, new teachers began advocating meditative practices of imagining or visualizing the Buddha, which further encouraged devotional Buddhism.

An effort to systematize diverse ways of understanding the Buddha developed in important Mahayana texts, famously known as the three bodies of the Buddha (*Trikaya*). These three represent three distinct ways to envision and to experience the Buddha. The first is the Buddha as initially conceived in Buddhism, the historical, earthly Buddha. By this time, however, the expansion of the Buddhist understanding of the cosmos meant that there might be multiple Buddhas, not just in the past but simultaneously teaching the dharma in wholly different and remote world systems. In addition to this way of understanding the Buddha, a second form was derived from descriptions of religious experience in which the Buddha would have appeared to an advanced bodhisattva or anyone else. Accounts of visionary experiences of this sort aided the development of devotional practice.

A third way that the Buddha might be present to human experience was more abstract. Referred to as the "dharma body," this was regarded as the highest vision of the Buddha, identical to the experience of awakening to the true nature of reality. The Buddha's teaching as presented in the Mahayana sutras claimed that emptiness was the ultimate nature of all things, that is, that they have no fixed essence, that they interfuse with all other things, and that this enormous cosmic process of interdependent transformation is unimaginably beautiful to behold. Seeing the Buddha as the dharma body is seeing everything as the Buddha, a vision that penetrates the surface of things to see the Buddha within them. Although human beings might get a glimpse of this vision, a comprehensive awareness of this reality is how the Buddha's own experience was imagined.

There were certainly Buddhists who were critical of the emergence of devotional tendencies within Buddhism, and this debate continues today. But the liberal attitude toward this development within Mahayana Buddhism was an aspect of the way they thought of the Mahayana as the great vehicle, the all-inclusive form of Buddhism that was great enough to encompass religious ideas and practices of people in all classes and communities who might be less likely to have the time or inclination to engage in meditation or philosophical reflection. The great vehicle was thought capable of absorbing these alternative modes of religious expression and employing their own virtues on behalf of awakening for everyone.

As a result of this expansion of the Mahayana dharma, images of different Buddhas in different world systems arose within devotional and meditative contexts. Visualizing these Buddhas, each with his own iconographic elements and symbols, became an important religious practice and helped to expand the devotional side of Buddhism. Amitabha Buddha, Vairocana Buddha, and the Healing Buddha are among the most prominent of these and today the most widely represented in Buddhist art. Images of "celestial bodhisattvas" evolved to parallel the diverse Buddhas, particular archetypical images of bodhisattvas representing the primary virtues of Buddhism, such as compassion, wisdom, and the next Buddha-to-be, Maitreya.

3.20. What elements of teaching are distinct to the Tantric tradition?

Tantric Buddhism, or Vajrayana, constituted a new phase in the development of Mahayana Buddhism wherein Buddhism was extended and transformed through its encounter with other Indian religions, most notably Hindu Saivism. As we noted earlier, Tantra was a pan-Indian religious movement in that it introduced religious ideas and practices that all traditions absorbed to greater or lesser degrees. Although Tantric ideas were clearly transformative among Buddhists, these Vajrayana innovations are to be found primarily in the domain of spiritual practice rather than in the teachings themselves, and we will address these innovations in the chapter on Buddhist practice.

Tantric Buddhist thought, however, focused on specific Mahayana ideas and extended them by applying them to aspects of life that had not occurred to earlier Buddhists. Many of these ideas were derived from the principal Mahayana sutras as they came to be developed in the Buddhist philosophical schools of Madhyamaka and Yogacara. As with Mahayana Buddhism, the principal theme was *emptiness*.

Emptiness provided the philosophical justification for the extensive practice of nondualism in Tantric Buddhism. Overcoming rigid mental dualities became the primary practice of spiritual transformation. The dualism between the sacred and the profane, both empty of any necessary exclusion of each other, could be psychologically overcome by practices that valorize the profane or degrade the sacred. The male/female gender duality was shown in the *Vimalakirti* sutra to be

empty of static meaning such that role reversals could be effectively practiced to liberating effects. Other dualities targeted
by Tantric nondualism were nirvana and samsara, the pure
and the impure, upper and lower classes, even the traditionally rigid boundary between monastic and lay Buddhists.
Although the early Mahayana theory of nondualism based on
emptiness was already pervasive, extensions of these ideas in
Tantric practice brought out applications of them that were not
previously visible.

Extending this line of thought, Tantric Buddhism made
greater use of the Mahayana concept of *skillful means*, the idea
that the liberating effects of emptiness would allow the development of techniques or methods for bringing psychological
transformation along more quickly. Tantric Buddhism was to
be an accelerated, direct path to the highest levels of Buddhist
realization.

A final idea that gives distinction to Tantric Buddhism is
the Mahayana concept of the *Buddha nature* to be found in all
living beings, or more broadly in all things. This Buddha nature
was symbolized as the womb or the embryo of Buddhahood,
the ground from which it comes into existence. It was also
imagined as a seed that when watered and cultivated would
sprout and grow into profound enlightenment. The seed of
awakening was to be found in all living beings. As such it also
had a role to play in debates about caste status in Buddhism,
whether there are any human beings who cannot be considered
capable of full awakening. This idea helped practitioners imagine Buddhist practice as the unfolding of an inner seed or
an innate potential rather than something alien that had to
be absorbed from outside the person. It made enlightenment
look more like a natural development than an extraordinary
transformation from one nature to another. Tantric Buddhists
made greater use of this early Mahayana idea than earlier
Buddhists had, and its influence in East Asian Buddhism—in
China, Korea, and Japan—is substantial. It also forms an important link between Tibetan and Mongolian Buddhism—the

primary locus of Tantric tradition—and these East Asian forms of Buddhism.

3.21. What are the basic teachings of devotional Buddhism?

This question is misleading in that it assumes that the devotional dimension of Buddhist practice can be easily separated from other teachings or that there is a distinct and separate sect of Buddhism in which these ideas are located. In fact, some form of devotion or reverence, as we have already seen, is a long-standing practice within almost all strands of Buddhism, and teachings related to these practices can be found in many Buddhist writings. The early ritual of "taking refuge in the Buddha, dharma, and sangha" already highlights this tendency. Nevertheless, it would be true to say that in early Buddhism and in many if not most lines of Buddhist tradition, ideas related to the worship of the Buddha would have either been subordinated to other, more prominent teachings or largely ignored. From the perspective of Western religions, in which devotion and worship of God is primary, the Buddhist pattern of reverence and devotion as a preliminary and subordinate dimension of religious practice is counterintuitive.

In response to this question, let's highlight historical moments in the tradition in which theistic elements did in fact become prominent for some or even many Buddhists and describe the teachings of one segment of Buddhism in which these devotional aspects became central to Buddhist thought and practice.

The *Lotus* sutra, composed around 200 CE, has become very influential in East Asian Buddhism. It develops a nuanced concept of the Buddha as the compassionate and omniscient Lord of our particular world system and does so in evocative religious parables that are both moving and memorable. The sutra begins with Gautama entering a deep state of meditation, at which point miracles and transcendent signs of the Buddha's omnipotence appear. The historical Gautama who once taught

Buddhism is now shown to be a temporary and partial incarnation of the absolute Buddha who appears in various guises in order to lure wayward human beings into the dharma. The Buddha explains to his audience that although he has taught many versions of Buddhism to people in different situations and capacities, in the end there is only one way to attain perfect enlightenment. That one way does not require meditation and philosophical sophistication but rather profound faith and an opportunity to be in the presence of the Buddha in another realm.

Another set of sutras, the *Land of Bliss* sutras, written about the same time as the *Lotus* sutra, has Gautama telling a story of a devout bodhisattva who took formal vows to create a heavenly realm devoid of all evil in which the inhabitants would inevitably experience immediate insight into the deepest teachings of the dharma. Gautama proclaims that this bodhisattva has now become Amitabha, or "Unlimited Light" Buddha, presiding over the newly created Land of Bliss. Furthermore, it is claimed that anyone, even the most ordinary of human beings, can be transported to this land at death by having fulfilled certain minimal conditions. Although these conditions differ in each version of the sutra, they include faith in the vows that have created the Land of Bliss, the sincere desire to be reborn there, and an effort to cultivate basic Buddhist virtues. One version of the sutra emphasizes the practice of chanting the name of Amitabha Buddha, which will help make one receptive to the grace of the Buddha, which was thought to enable rebirth in this heavenly realm.

Among the various kinds of Buddhism that have emphasized devotional practices over other, more traditional Buddhist practices is the Japanese True Pure Land sect (Jodo Shinshu) founded by Shinran in the early thirteenth century. Shinran was a Buddhist monk who, like the Christian reformer Martin Luther, was tormented by the belief that he did not deserve an afterlife in heaven, in this case, rebirth in the Land of Bliss. After decades of internal struggle, Shinran had a series of dreams that led him to teach a new form of Buddhism based on the *Land of Bliss* sutras. He advocated that for anyone in his sinful situation the best practice was to chant the *Nembutsu* (Hail to Amida, or Amitabha, Buddha), as had been recommended in the *Land of Bliss* sutras.

Emphasizing complete faith in the compassionate intention of the Buddha to open the Pure Land even to sinful human beings, Shinran taught that even one fully sincere chant would open a person's heart to the grace of the Buddha. Not only was the human effort to make oneself deserving of this destiny thought to be inadequate; it also showed a lack of faith in the compassionate grace of the Buddha, who vowed to extend access to the Land of Bliss regardless of whether it was deserved. Shinran contrasted "self power" Buddhist practices that failed to attain open humility with the "other power" practice of the *Nembutsu* wherein Amida Buddha empowered the joyful recitation of the name of the Buddha within the mind of the practitioner.

These examples of the teachings of devotional Buddhism disguise the extent to which the teachings are often subordinate to practices of devotion. But teachings establish the context in which these practices make sense to Buddhists and are essential in that role. Most Buddhists include a moment of devotional humility within the larger scope of their practice, regardless of what that practice entails. In that sense, the cultivation of reverence is one dimension of a full regime of Buddhist practice.

3.22. What are the primary teachings of Zen Buddhism, and what role do they play in Zen practice?

By its own account, Zen teachings focus initially on the Buddhist teachings themselves—a terse rejection of the way the Buddhist teachings had become yet another object of attachment and ego enhancement. Bodhidharma, the legendary founder of Chan or Zen, is credited with having founded Zen as:

A special tradition outside the sutras;
With no dependence on words and letters.
Directly pointing to the mind;
Seeing one's own nature and attaining Buddhahood.

Zen was proclaimed to function "outside the teachings of the sutras," without relying on language, because it points directly to the true nature of mind—no need for intermediary devices, no need to labor over the meaning of the sacred texts if through meditative practice you can see the Buddha nature right there in your own mind.

Scholarly knowledge of Buddhist teachings was sometimes scorned in Zen. That kind of access to the dharma was thought to obscure and undermine the deepest intent of the teachings: direct, unmediated awareness of one's own impermanence, dependence, and selflessness. So unlike most other types of Buddhism, Zen began its teachings with a powerful and ironic repudiation of the traditional role of the teachings. Scholarly relations to the dharma undermine the very possibility of awakening, they thought, and Zen was launched as a radical alternative to that way of being a Buddhist.

As we saw earlier, the word *zen* in Japanese, which is *chan* in Chinese and *seon* in Korean, means "meditation," and to a great extent this tradition has adamantly focused on the practice of meditation rather than on Buddhist teachings. But another way to look at this is to consider how the teachings of Zen always emerge in the context of meditative practice, and that the two are not as separable as they might appear to be. The theme of inseparability or nondualism is in fact the primary teaching of Zen, and the number of practical ways it appears in Zen is perhaps the greatest contribution this tradition makes to Buddhism. A famous story in the *Vimalakirti* sutra was very influential in establishing this typically Zen focus. In that story, Vimalakirti, a radical and insightful lay Buddhist, asks his many bodhisattva guests to each say what they think nondualism is. Each offers a fascinating example of how reality isn't divided into separate, unrelated categories, and how each thing is in fact linked to its opposite. We get a glimpse into nondualism from a wide variety of perspectives. Then the bodhisattva guests ask for Vimalakirti's version of nondualism, and in response he sits there silently, refusing to allow dualistic language to break the silence of nondual presence.

Here are a few examples of how the Mahayana Buddhist teaching of nondualism emerges in Zen:

- Zen teachers stress that meditation practice and all of the rest of everyday life are not separate. All acts are practice. Zen monks are taught to regard everything they do as further engagement in meditation: manual labor, eating, bathing, everything.
- Buddha nature, the capacity for enlightenment inherent in all people, is present in all things. Soto Zen master Dogen teaches how "grass, trees, the land, all teach the dharma" and that to "forget oneself is to be enlightened by all things." Since the Buddha nature is everywhere, anything may be the catalyst for awakening.
- Awakening is the sudden welling up within you of your own Buddha nature since in Zen teachings you already are the Buddha and need not be fundamentally transformed in order to recognize what is already true. Enlightenment is not a distant goal. The only task is to realize its ubiquitous presence.
- The practice of meditation seeking enlightenment and the realization of enlightenment are one and the same. That is, when you sit in meditation you are expressing your own internal Buddha nature, showing or demonstrating it, not preparing for its eventual emergence.

• Authentic art and authentic religion are nondual. Artistic insight and spiritual insight are regarded as essentially the same and held in positions of highest honor. Based on this realization, many if not most Zen masters have also been advanced participants in one or another artistic practice: painting, calligraphy, garden design, and poetry, among others.

The practice of silent meditation dominates Zen temples and monasteries. But precisely because words are so scarce in Zen they are accordingly more important, not less. Language in Zen is more powerful, more ponderous, more strategic, and more directed to insight than in any other setting where words flow easily and always. Since the chatter of everyday life is not permitted in Zen temples, when words do emerge they are taken with the utmost seriousness. Zen teachers give "dharma talks" in which they strive to provide direct access to the state of mind that is sought in Zen. Rather than speak about it they attempt to *bespeak* the dharma, to open a space for an experience of it to occur through those words. This effort gives rise to very unusual language, often paradoxical and puzzling. Such language is assigned to practitioners so that it can be traced back to the awakened state of mind from which it has arisen. Much Zen practice entails meditation on these spoken words of famous teachers—essentially the sutras of Zen—in spite of the slogan proclaiming "No dependence on words and letters."

Finally, Zen teachings include reflections on what is called "mind-to-mind transmission," the idea that since true awakening is not passed down as the mastery of certain teachings it is instead passed directly from the mind of a Zen master to the mind of a student when the student also attains the status of authentication as an awakened Zen master. Early in the Zen tradition this is illustrated in an apocryphal story about the Buddha presenting dharma talks to his disciples. On one occasion, rather than discussing Buddhist ideas, he simply holds up a flower. This baffles everyone, except the monk Mahakasyapa, who smiles an enlightened smile of recognition. At that moment, the Buddha is thought to have passed the dharma to Mahakasyapa without a word being spoken. Similarly, Zen masters employ skillful means to awaken disciples without burdening their minds with abstruse ideas that obscure more than clarify.

3.23. What are the primary rules, virtues, and vices in Buddhist morality?

Early Buddhist sutras situate morality as one of three fundamental areas of religious practice. Good conduct (*sila*) was regarded as a prerequisite for any higher aspiration and was thus thought to be necessary before the other two—meditation and wisdom—could begin in earnest. Initially this meant that a person should engage in moral training to distinguish between wholesome or healthy acts, which are motivated by nonattachment, kindness, and discernment, and unhealthy acts, which draw motivation from greed, hatred, or delusion. Once this distinction is sufficiently clear, training concentrates on how to prefer health over its opposite, especially when unhealthy acts are powerfully alluring.

For most Buddhists, this training begins with the Five Precepts, which are to be practiced with dedicated intention, in spite of lapses that might occur. The precepts are moral teachings that provide practitioners with guidelines to assist in imagining what the shape of an admirable Buddhist life can be. These five apply to lay people as well as monks and nuns, although monastic life called for another five precepts in addition to the first five and the hundreds of guidelines outlined in the monastic code of conduct. The first five are (1) to refrain from harming living beings, which specifically means no killing of any sentient life; (2) to refrain from taking what has not been given, a prohibition on stealing; (3) to refrain from sexual misconduct, most particularly adultery but extendable to other sexual prohibitions; (4) to refrain from false speech, not just lying but other related verbal abuses; and (5) to refrain from intoxicants that induce heedlessness, which applies to alcohol and drugs that reduce mental clarity and give rise to unwholesome and careless behavior.

Although lists of prohibitions and virtues are a substantial part of Buddhist moral teachings, the overall emphasis is on the practitioner's personal engagement in moral training. This training includes exercises of self-cultivation that shape motivations, build healthy habits of action, and develop a kind of moral clarity that is related to wisdom. Whether or not practitioners think of it this way, this spiritual training aims at the realization of selflessness (or no-self), a sense of interdependence (dependent arising), and an awareness of transformative possibilities for individuals and communities (impermanence). Therefore, although Buddhist rules are an explicit dimension of morality, the focus is less on adherence to rules than on training oneself to recognize one's own hidden inclinations toward greed, hatred, and delusion and to begin to build personal habits that avoid these motivations in favor of motives conducive to a healthy life of nonattachment, friendliness, and clarity of mind.

With those provisions in mind, we can examine several lists of Buddhist virtues. While mindfulness meditation techniques focus on simply observing what is there to be seen, other meditation techniques concentrate on ideals of character with personal change in mind. An early and important group of noble characteristics is the Four Immeasurables, or the Four Divine Abodes: lovingkindness, compassion, sympathetic joy, and equanimity. Lovingkindness is the aspiration to develop and maintain feelings of goodwill toward all beings, the desire that they be happy and healthy. As one develops that sense of goodwill, the basis of compassion is established. Compassion is the desire for an end to suffering for all beings, including oneself but ultimately everyone in equal proportion. Sympathetic joy is the aspiration to be as happy and as satisfied with the success and good fortune of others as one would be with one's own good fortune. Another's joy becomes one's own since selflessness ultimately affirms the value of all beings equally. Finally, in order to modulate the depth of feeling that the first three might generate, equanimity affirms the necessity of balance and unattached proportion. Suffering and joy are inevitable aspects of life for all living beings, and reconciliation to that truth is the strength of resilience to sustain practitioners in the selfless practice of the other ideal qualities.

Next let us examine the Six Perfections mentioned earlier, the six dimensions of human character considered to constitute the bodhisattva's enlightenment in early Mahayana Buddhism. Accounts of these six show them to be both areas of contemplative training and perfections, aspirational ideals that one can only hope to embody in some degree. First among them is generosity, the perfection of giving. Aspiring bodhisattvas meditate on acts of giving. They picture themselves giving selflessly in hopes that these mental exercises will begin to instill natural inclinations to give and to be helpful when opportunities arise. Second is moral training. Learn to do unto others as you would want them to do unto you. Refrain from acting in such a way that others are harmed or thwarted by your acts. Third is the perfection of tolerance or patience. This entails learning nonattachment to your own views, your own preferences and ways of doing things, so that you become more and more able to accommodate differences between different kinds of people with different views, aspirations, and problems to overcome.

Fourth, the path of the bodhisattva requires energy and effort, the strength of character to not give up when things go badly but to push ahead thoughtfully and energetically in life no matter what happens. Fifth, the perfection of meditation is involved in the cultivation of all of the foregoing traits of character. Meditation is the central practice for Buddhists, enabling the gradual cultivation of character. It entails concentration and mindfulness as well as specific mental exercises to gradually absorb these Buddhist ideals into one's character and to embody them in everyday life. Finally, wisdom is the loftiest dimension of Buddhist self-cultivation and is implied in all of the other perfections. Generosity or morality or tolerance without wisdom will always be limited. The Buddhist claim, then, is that without wisdom your understanding and actualization of other ideals of character will ultimately undermine them.

Negative versions of Buddhist virtue lists are also prominent in the tradition. Accompanying the Three Poisons of greed, hatred, and delusion are lists such as the Five Hindrances, specifically sensual desire, ill will, tiredness and lassitude, excitement and depression, and debilitating, fearful doubt. Each set of virtues and vices functions as a theme for meditative practice. These are contemplative exercises in which practitioners imagine specific situations in life, and then picture themselves acting in ways that they would hope to act when similar situations actually arise. Repetitive mental training was thought to develop habits of discernment and action so that when situations come up in life these more enlightened responses might emerge.

3.24. What is Buddhist enlightenment? Is that what nirvana means?

Following what has come to be known as the European Age of Enlightenment, the word *enlightenment* was selected in various Western languages to name what Asian Buddhists had regarded as the highest conceivable achievement for a human being, the most exalted state of human existence. The most important early Buddhist word for this was *nirvana*, and through this lengthy route of cross-cultural events, *enlightenment* and *nirvana* became synonyms in Western writing about Buddhism. Let's begin with what Buddhists have to say about nirvana.

The story of the Buddha's life reached its apex when in his midthirties he had a life-altering experience of nirvana. The word *nirvana* means the "extinguishing" or "blowing out" of a flame or fire, and in the early Buddhist sutras focused on the Buddha's nirvana experience this is portrayed as the extinction of the fires of craving and attachment. The Buddha is freed from the craving inherent in greed and hatred, but also freed from the delusions that give rise to this craving. Delusion is overcome through clarity and insight, a direct awareness of reality made possible by freedom from the compulsions entailed in craving. Delusion and craving stand in a reciprocal relation, each sustaining the other, and their release in the experience of nirvana undermines the foundations of both. As a consequence of this liberation, the Buddha is imagined to be beyond suffering, dwelling in a state of profound equanimity and balance.

Early sutras use the word *nirvana* to refer not just to one life-changing moment but also to the state of mind in which the Buddha or anyone else dwells for the remainder of life. This state of nirvana is characterized by four immeasurable attributes: compassion, lovingkindness, sympathetic joy, and equanimity. It is also stable, an inner state of security, calm, and peace, free of the disturbance and oppression that compulsions imply. Nirvana is regarded as the only truly healthy state of being—combining mental clarity, magnanimity, freedom, and peace—no matter what terrible condition one's bodily existence might be in. From stories of the long life of the Buddha after his initial nirvana experience, we can see that this state of mind is fully involved in the world rather than aloof, as though dwelling in some other world.

In addition to these worldly characteristics of nirvana, however, there are references to another form of nirvana that begins when an awakened person dies. Nirvana "without remainder," or *parinirvana*, is no longer conditioned by the Five Aggregates or components of a human life and is imagined as the extinction of all cycles of rebirth. This state is called "deathless," the "unconditioned realm," in which all the unstable, out-of-balance conditions of life come to an end in perfect peace. To probing questions about where an enlightened person goes after death the Buddha remains silent. The early Buddhist idea is that those who enter parinirvana cannot be said to exist nor not to exist, nor both nor neither. To claim existence is to fall into the Buddhist error of eternalism. To claim nonexistence is to plunge into the opposite error of nihilism. As we saw earlier, Buddhism claims to be a Middle Path through these errors of judgment.

Nirvana is thus beyond human imagination, beyond linguistic description, beyond the logic that applies in worldly existence. Nirvana is not a place, not another world, not anything else that our minds can conjure. Hence the Buddha's smile, and silence, as well as his insistence that there are much more pressing matters to consider: how to free yourself from compulsions, delusions, and pointless suffering. In other words, if you live wisely, if you live a wholesome, healthy life free of the emotional compulsions of craving, you can afford to let the afterlife take care of itself. And if you don't live such a life, no amount of pondering your destiny in other worlds will help.

But the meaning of Buddhist enlightenment is not limited to these early Indian Buddhist reflections on nirvana. Indeed, even in Indian Buddhism other ways of imagining the most exalted forms of human life come into prominence over time. In fact, the metaphor of awakening (*bodhi*) and synonyms for it in other languages were more frequently used than *nirvana*. In Mahayana Buddhism, the awakened bodhisattva postpones nirvana in preference for a life of continual rebirth in order to assist in the liberation of all living beings. Mahayana writings describe the life of the bodhisattva in contrast to the Theravada arhat, who seeks nirvana. This ungenerous caricature of the early Buddhist quest for nirvana depicts it as otherworldly monastic seclusion, an escape from the lives ordinary human beings face, and in this respect as a failure of compassion. In its place new Mahayana ways of understanding the highest ideals of Buddhism emerge.

As Buddhism moved into other cultures with existing ideas about the apex of human life, and as the long history of Buddhism unfolded, Buddhist ways of understanding its highest ideals evolved, and with them people's experiences of enlightenment. There are Tantric ways of picturing ultimate goals in life, Zen ways, Buddhist devotional ways, and many more. If we take this diverse history seriously, we eventually come to the conclusion that enlightenment is not a preexistent ideal set for all time, but rather a vision of exalted ideals that can't help but evolve through various circumstances over time.

One Zen reference to enlightenment captures this sense of contingency and impermanence. In it a Zen master proclaims that if any of his disciples ever attains something equivalent to his enlightenment, that student will need to "have gone beyond the master." This means that each emerging Zen master would experience a unique, unprecedented awakening, because each would be faced with somewhat different barriers, somewhat different inclinations, orientations, and life experiences. And in this way, every new Zen master would extend the tradition in some unique direction, adding something new to the repertoire of Buddhist enlightenment. As Buddhists have claimed since the beginning, nothing has a fixed and static essence, and everything unfolds differently under newly emerging conditions. Practitioners can thereby be enlightened about the status of enlightenment and release emotionally laden attachments to particular images of enlightenment while nevertheless engaging is this quest with all available energy.

4

BUDDHIST PRACTICES

4.1. What is the relationship between Buddhist teachings and the practice of Buddhism?

Buddhist practices are spiritual activities or exercises intentionally undertaken to cultivate the mental states and ideal ways of living that are articulated in the teachings. The teachings explain what Buddhism is about in theoretical terms. Practices are designed to actualize those goals, to weave them into the lives of Buddhists in practical ways. Both are important. But by and large the tendency throughout Buddhist history has been to place somewhat more emphasis on what you do than on what you believe.

Some forms of Buddhism, Zen most famously, are occasionally scornful of Buddhist theory, thereby de-emphasizing concern about the correctness of Buddhist beliefs. Ideas were thought sometimes to clutter the mind and to stand in the way of seeing how things really are. Although Buddhist philosophy holds an important place in the tradition, the practical orientation, going all the way back to the Buddha himself, warns against overemphasizing the thinking side of Buddhism. Life as we ordinarily live it is riddled with confusion and suffering. Only action can change that. Think clearly and practically about what to do. Then just do it.

The guiding insight here is that in shaping the quality of your life, what you do is more significant than what you believe, even if both have a vital role. That is why early Buddhists adopted the image of Buddhism as a path to be traveled and explored, an image of activity and movement. And although dichotomies between true and false and between good and evil are certainly important in Buddhism, much more significant and more frequently expressed are dichotomies between skillful and unskillful practices, between wholesome and unwholesome actions. From a long-standing Buddhist point of view, until we have engaged seriously in transformative practices, our beliefs will invariably be deluded, motivated by self-centered, immature, and unwholesome concerns. They will be infused to some degree with the Three Poisons of greed, hatred, and delusion.

Through transformative practice, Buddhists believe, the perspective from which beliefs are formulated and held can be skillfully altered to make possible an awakened vision of the world grounded in compassion and wisdom. A reciprocal relationship between the teachings and practice has been nurtured throughout the tradition. The teachings are essential in providing direction, rationale, and motivation for Buddhist practices. But practice is primary since only practical engagement can bring enduring change, and the focus of Buddhism is on transformation.

4.2. How is Buddhist practice related to karma and the goal of enlightenment?

Karma is a theory that articulates what Buddhists see as an inescapable link between what someone does and who he or she becomes. What becomes of you in life, what kind of person you turn out to be, depends on what you have done and the cumulative effect of all of your choices and actions. Sometimes karma is thought to be related to particular incidences in life: How did you address the homeless person who approached you begging for some food? What ethical choices did you make as a business person? How did you treat your parents? Your children? Every incident in life is thought to have a karmic judgment written into it, and in every act, large or small, we reveal exactly who we are.

The Buddhist idea of karma encompasses not only the momentous choices we make but also the millions of small habitual choices that are equally weighty in the construction of our character. Buddhists recognize that our lives are profoundly shaped by habits that we reenact daily, by patterns of behavior that we perform without being particularly aware of them. Everyday actions and failures of action mold us into who we are over time. From this perspective, thousands of small choices—just doing what we have always done—can have a much more significant impact on our character than any one momentous decision.

So Buddhist practice and karma are irrevocably linked. The quality of what we do, the frequency and integrity with which we do it, and the connections we draw between our practices and the rest of our lives—all are essential to the Buddhist understanding of karmic self-sculpting. Mindful, fully self-aware moments of choice are moments of freedom. Buddhist practice is centrally concerned with cultivating and developing this freedom.

How, then, are practice and karma related to enlightenment? Buddhists understand that enlightenment, or awakening, is a rare human achievement that makes its appearance for very clear reasons. As the teachings on dependent arising explain, nothing arises or occurs until the appropriate conditions are in place. Enlightenment depends on a person's having undertaken disciplines of mindful behavior to an extent great enough to undermine human tendencies toward greed, hatred, and delusion. Through daily practice and purposeful training of the mind, human beings establish the conditions conducive to enlightened awareness. Karma is related to practice as the natural and logical outcome of a person's acts, habits, and ways of living. When these acts, habits, and ways of living are being intentionally shaped by a discipline of practice, karmic conditions for the emergence of enlightenment are gradually being satisfied.

4.3. What aspects of life are thought to be affected by Buddhist practice?

Buddhism is a comprehensive way of life that calls for the gradual transformation of virtually all aspects of human awareness and behavior. Therefore, nothing a person does is fully outside the scope or range of Buddhist practice. Ideally, then, practices affect life in all of its dimensions. One of the early Buddhist sutras says that Buddhist striving takes place in three broad domains: good conduct, meditative concentration, and wisdom.

These three areas of discipline were often thought to follow in that specific order, so that the first order of business for a Buddhist—good conduct—would be to begin observing one's own conduct and then altering some of those patterns of behavior in light of Buddhist ideals. Good conduct is morally admirable behavior, unselfish actions, and generosity in dealings with others. Early Buddhist texts explain that until we can live peacefully and in harmony with others around us we are in no position to learn deep concentration or to embody wisdom. Once good-conduct practices have begun to affect our patterns of behavior, we can begin the practice of meditation in order to develop the skills of focus, mindfulness, and concentration. After these skills are developed to a certain degree, another kind of meditative practice specifically targeting wisdom can begin. These wisdom practices focus on the Buddhist teachings of impermanence, no-self, and human suffering and aim to instill Buddhist insights of this kind into the most instinctual levels of the human mind.

A slightly more detailed discussion of the full scope of Buddhist practice occurs in the teachings of the Eightfold Path, the last of the Buddhist Four Noble Truths. The way to deal with suffering in life and to undermine the cravings and delusions that give rise to suffering is the practice of these eight distinct disciplines. People who cultivate themselves successfully in these eight areas will have laid the foundations for Buddhist awakening. The Eightfold Path encompasses:

1. Appropriate views—understanding the causes of suffering in life, the prevalence of change, the fact that all things depend upon other things, the lack of a permanent, static self, and other prominent insights.
2. Appropriate intentions—intentions guided by habitual greed, hatred, and delusion are to be replaced by wise and compassionate intentions that channel human choices and acts in enlightening ways.
3. Appropriate speech—the cultivation of mindful communication so that words spoken are truthful, peaceful, and conducive to effective and compassionate interaction between ourselves and others.
4. Appropriate actions—consciously developing patterns of behavior that are not harmful or demeaning to others and the environment but are instead open, helpful, and generous.
5. Appropriate livelihood—becoming mindful that although all people need to procure the basic material conditions of life (food, shelter, clothing, etc.), some ways of doing this are harmful to the community and the natural world, while others support the development and enhancement of healthy communal relations.
6. Appropriate effort—the cultivation of discipline in one's life such that intentions, decisions, and plans are carefully enacted, and unhealthy counterforces are curtailed or undermined.
7. Appropriate mindfulness—developing the sustained capacity of awareness to pay close attention at all times to what is really going on both within you and beyond you.
8. Appropriate concentration—the scattered, dull, distracted states of mind that are natural for all of us are replaced through meditative discipline by pointed concentration and sharp focus.

If you look closely at these eight areas of disciplined practice, they appear to cover virtually all aspects of life. Some of them have to do with good conduct (3, 4, 5), some with meditative concentration (6, 7, 8), and some with wisdom (1, 2). The primary point is that because Buddhist enlightenment constitutes a fundamental transformation of human character, skillful interventions in the form of explicit practices are useful in every area of life. In most cases these begin and end in some form of Buddhist meditation, the practice and discipline most often associated with Buddhism.

4.4. What is Buddhist meditation?

Meditation is certainly the most recognizable of all Buddhist practices. But Buddhists didn't singlehandedly invent meditation. Meditation was a pan-Indian invention practiced in some way by participants in at least several different religious traditions. Their influence on other religions around the world continues to expand today as meditation practices go global.

Recent writers on Buddhism warn readers not to overemphasize the importance of meditation in Buddhism. After all, one need only travel extensively in Asia to see that most Buddhists appear not to meditate at all. And historians today can verify that this has probably been true throughout the long history of Buddhism. While monks, nuns, and small groups of especially interested lay people have continued the practice of meditation throughout Buddhist history, the majority of other Buddhists have not.

In saying this, however, we should be cautious about what we mean by meditation. Probably the earliest and most frequently used word for meditation in Sanskrit is *bhavana*, "bringing into being" or "developing" the spiritual dimension of human character, clearly a term with broad connotations. In this sense meditation encompasses a variety of methods to cultivate and support the awakening of wisdom and compassion, the ultimate goals of

Buddhism. So, while our image of meditation is typically specific and somewhat narrow, Buddhists have been able to see how meditation encompasses such practices as devotional exercises, moral self-scrutiny, and reflections on Buddhist teachings. In that sense, anyone who takes time out of ordinary life to engage in some mental or spiritual practice engages in meditation. These are all ways to gather oneself momentarily into a different state of mind, a state characterized by mindfulness, composure, clarity, or vision.

The goal of Buddhist meditation is to restore the mind to a state of fundamental clarity and composure—one that it naturally embodies but which can be difficult to achieve because of obstructions. There are various lists of these obstructions, but the most widely known is called the Five Hindrances. They are sensual desire or craving, ill will, tiredness, the extremes of excitement and depression, and debilitating doubt. These tendencies are thought to hinder all human undertakings, but particularly those of a spiritual character.

To counter these negative forces in the mind, early sutras picture the Buddha singling out two contemplative qualities of mind that could be developed in meditation and that were closely aligned with the experience of nirvana. The first is "calm abiding" (*samatha*), which includes meditative techniques that concentrate and unify the mind into a deeply stable composure. The second is "insight" (*vipassana*), which encompasses a variety of investigative techniques for exploring the true nature of all states of mind and all experiences of the world.

4.5. What are the primary forms or styles of Buddhist meditation?

Having developed over many centuries, the range and variety of Buddhist meditation techniques or styles are so great that it is difficult to grasp them all. But here are four broad types of contemplative practice that can serve as a guide:

- Concentration. This type of meditation is frequently considered a precursor for other types in that calming or stilling the flighty and otherwise distracted mind clears the way for other types of mental exercise. Buddhists have been insightful in recognizing the extent to which the uncontrolled torrent of thoughts and emotions to which human beings are typically subject is highly dysfunctional. Introspective examination of ordinary mental processes brought Buddhists to see the extent of our mental agitation—how unable we are to focus and how often we lack the internal freedom to determine what our minds will or won't do. This is our default state of mind, as disconnected and unchosen images and thoughts rush through our minds from minute to minute and hour to hour. Concentration practices aim to overcome mental distraction and over time to expand our capacity to focus on something purposefully without losing that control. In addition to being a preparatory exercise for other forms of meditation, concentration can also be practiced at the most rarified levels of human experience. Buddhists used the word *samadhi* to name the ideal depth of concentration that they saw embodied in enlightened beings.
- Mindfulness. A second category of Buddhist meditation practices engages in internal observation. Mindfulness exercises teach practitioners to become directly aware of the contents of experience as they arise in the mind, develop, and then disappear, without analysis, interpretation, and critical judgment complicating this basic level of experience. The only element of will or intention involved is that of observation: the desire to see what the present moment entails both internally and externally on its own without imposing anything else upon it. This is a cultivated capacity for awareness, acceptance,

and appreciation—just seeing what is there without our projections. One additional facet of mindfulness practice allows practitioners to label or name the contents of experience before letting them fade into the mental background. Through open observation meditators can see and label an unnecessary thought about food, and then let it go; observe a feeling of resentment, and then release it; experience a moment of fear or self-doubt, label it as such, and then release it. The act of labeling allows practitioners to become conscious of what otherwise occurs to them unconsciously. This exercise shows practitioners what it is that cycles through their minds as well as how compulsive these experiences typically are.

- Reflective insight. A third type of Buddhist meditation cultivates insight into the most fundamental elements of human experience by means of analytical inquiry. Focusing initially on three elements of human experience that Buddhists understood to be most critical, meditators investigate the impermanence of all things, the ultimate lack of static selfhood, and the extent to which suffering and our different responses to suffering shape human lives. Other topics for insight meditation vary according to differences in the lives of practitioners. The goal of this practice is freedom from delusion and compulsion through direct awareness of the true nature of human experience. Attaining insight into the processes underlying our lives is thought to give rise to liberation from unwholesome and unskillful ways of living.
- Constructive or Developmental. A fourth category of meditation among Buddhists is active in cultivating new dispositions, habits, and presuppositions that are judged to be wholesome or skillful in life and that replace old habits of mind that have caused unnecessary suffering. These exercises target particular mental and emotional qualities of character that are open to development, strengthening, and improvement. Unlike nonjudgmental mindfulness observations, these meditations follow from

judgments about which habits of mind are conducive to lives of openness and wisdom, and which are not. They seek to alter the mind by implanting qualities of character that are healthy and wise rather than personally destructive, qualities such as patience, gratitude, courage, compassion, humility, and forgiveness. This transformation occurs through internal visualization and repetition. By visualizing yourself reacting to an event with patience and forgiveness rather than with resentment and anger, as you might have previously, and by repeating this sequence many times, you gradually alter the default response that had previously been dominant and destructive.

Classical manuals of meditation and modern commentaries describe transitions that typically occur as Buddhists become proficient in meditation. One of these is that the judgment that naturally occurs early in meditation practice about whether the experience of it is pleasant or unpleasant slowly begins to shift. Meditators become interested in that very judgment and in the contrast in all of our experiences between the pleasant and the unpleasant. The unpleasant becomes as interesting to the serious meditator as the pleasant, and this kind of interest in the basic character of mind undermines earlier habits that expend all energy toward the pursuit of the pleasant and the abolition of the unpleasant.

This example also shows another transformation that occurs through the ongoing practice of meditation. Gradually a space develops between what happens to a person and that person's response to it. This space affords new levels of freedom to choose between possible responses to situations and events in life. Prior to contemplative practice, we simply respond to a particular type of event in the habitual, unintentional ways we have in the past. Meditative practice consciously develops alternatives to those patterns of action and enlarges the gap between stimulus and response just enough to allow us to choose a healthier response. The goal in this meditative exercise is freedom, freedom to resist ingrained but destructive mental and behavioral patterns and the freedom to insert in their place a carefully chosen alternative.

One final example of a change that is thought to occur with greater experience in meditation is a movement from intentional, planned activity toward a greater degree of open receptivity. At first, the effort required to meditate is huge; it requires strong will and determination along with an explicit plan for what it is that you will do while meditating. But in all four of the types of meditation chronicled above, a shift may occur over time in which very little willpower and determination are required and in which something of great importance is disclosed through the highly evolved mental postures of receptivity and openness. In this more refined state of openness, meditators get glimpses of things as they are on their own, without the imposition of human will and determination shaping them in advance to align with their own desires and perspectives. The deepest states of meditation are described as these experiences of "release" and "letting go."

4.6. What do Buddhist practitioners do in meditation?

The variety of Buddhist meditation exercises is initially quite puzzling. But this same variety is also illuminating, giving us a glimpse of both the inexhaustible potential of meditation practice and the extent to which Buddhist history is one lengthy and sophisticated extension of this basic practice. To get a sense of this scope imagine a meditator repeating a word or phrase as a meditation exercise, visualizing a troubling situation in order to rework internal response patterns, imagining the Buddha as a deity, observing tensions and obstructions in the body, listening to all available sounds in the present moment, dwelling on a Zen master's verbal riddle, contemplating a sutra passage, attending to internal respiration processes, or just sitting, doing nothing at all! All of these activities and hundreds more form the repertoire of Buddhist meditation. Buddhist teachers often prescribe a particular meditation exercise in order to suit the inclinations and temperament of a particular student. The general categories of meditation described above provide an overview of possibilities, but here are a few concrete examples:

- Almost invariably introductions to Buddhist meditation begin with *mindfulness of breathing*, a concentration exercise in which meditators place all of their attention on the body's respiratory processes. Practitioners are instructed to feel the abdomen expand and contract with the flexing and release of the diaphragm. Often the instruction is simply to count each breath up to ten and then to begin again. Meditators are asked not to force or prescribe any particular pattern of respiration—no analysis, judgments of quality, or efforts to improve—but just to observe the body do the rhythmic, respiratory dance that it has already done for many years without instruction or quality control. When the mind wanders off to other thoughts or feelings, as it invariably does, the meditator is asked to gently return to observe that breath and then the next. This simple exercise—which is not so simple in practice—is by far the most common Buddhist meditation, not just among beginners but among advanced practitioners as well.
- Another widely performed Buddhist meditation is *taking refuge*. Used by monks and nuns since the earliest eras of Buddhism, this practice has also come to be important for lay practitioners. It involves repeating a simple formula and visualizing each image: "I take refuge in the Buddha, I take refuge in the dharma, and I take refuge in the sangha." Taking refuge means turning oneself over, leaning upon something for support, acknowledging the importance of whatever it is that one takes refuge in. It is also something like a vow of conviction, a statement of determination. Taking refuge in the Buddha entails a commitment to the first teacher and to all teachers who follow in that path. Taking refuge in the dharma means

dedicating oneself to learning Buddhist teachings and embodying them in everyday life. Taking refuge in the sangha involves a commitment to one's community in terms of both receiving support and providing it to others. These phrases are either repeated silently or spoken along with others in unison. The idea is that repetition leads to actualization and to the embodiment of commitment and confidence.

- Imagine a word that reflects a quality of mind that you want to experience right now and to cultivate more deeply into your character, say, *balance, energy, patience, courage,* or *compassion.* Meditators then repeat that word silently with every in-breath, visualizing that quality of character entering their body along with the oxygen. In the exhalation, they imagine all forces working in the opposite direction exiting the body along with the lungful of air—all imbalance, impatience, and so on. They further picture that positive quality penetrating and pervading their entire being and from there radiating out to others. This meditation practice can focus on the negative just as well, targeting destructive emotions such as anger, resentment, or greed in order to let them go.

- A mindfulness practice focused on the status and sequence of one's own thoughts is widely practiced. Meditators simply observe the appearance and subsequent disappearance of thoughts as they move through the mind, one after another. Without judgment or analysis, they watch random thoughts come and go like effervescent bubbles, sometimes just labeling each of them as a thought. The practice aims to allow disidentification with one's thoughts, as though they just arise and pass away on their own without the need for a thinker to initiate their arrival and departure. Since we naturally identify closely with the contents of our mind and are thus unable to loosen their hold on us, this practice helps turn the intense drama of invading thoughts into something lighter and less dramatic, with uplifting therapeutic benefits.

- From the earliest documents of Buddhism come a number of meditations aimed at developing feelings of compassion for others. One variant of these is called *the exchange of self and others* and was recommended by Shantideva, an enormously influential medieval Mahayana monk. The exercises play on the Buddhist experience of no-self and the selfless actions that arise from an in-depth embodiment of this central Buddhist insight. The author asks meditators to focus on the thought that other people are basically like us—they strive for happiness and they suffer just like we do. Shantideva asks us why we invariably prioritize our own suffering and expend so little energy alleviating the suffering of others. He pushes this reasoning further and further so that meditators see more and more clearly that they aren't deserving of the special treatment they habitually give themselves. Practitioners move through these carefully orchestrated thoughts until finally Shantideva seems to almost shout at them, "Hey, Mind, make the resolution 'I am bound to others'! From now on you must have no other concern than the welfare of all beings." This meditation pushes the mind through analytical reasoning to the conclusion that all people, including but not especially ourselves, deserve our compassion. The repetition of these thoughts is meant to develop what was initially a mere thought into a deep instinctual feeling of connection with and compassion for others.
- Buddhist devotional meditations are employed extensively in some Buddhist communities. One of these, in what is called Pure Land Buddhism, has practitioners repeat the phrase "Homage to Amida Buddha" over and over. As they do, meditators gradually learn to identify it not as their own prayer or their own religious practice but as the effects of the grace of the Buddha arising in them. They open themselves to feel the gift of gratitude, allowing it to intensify into moments of joy, ease, and peace. Practitioners' own action is limited to

surrendering self-serving attitudes, turning themselves over to the Buddha nature working subtly within them. This practice is meant to bring the no-self realization at the heart of Buddhism into active experience through an awareness of the Buddha's presence.

Not only are there hundreds more, but new meditative exercises are being created all the time. These few give you a small sampler of Buddhist styles of meditation.

4.7. Why is bodily posture considered important in the practice of meditation?

Although meditation is ultimately a mental exercise, Buddhist meditation teachers have long maintained that bodily posture is essential as a foundation for mental and spiritual practice. The basic posture requirement is that the meditator's spine must be in alignment, neither leaning forward nor arching backward, but in a position of balance. In this posture the spine is not straight exactly, but slightly and gracefully curved in alignment with the body's natural curvature. The rationale for this posture is the need for bodily relaxation. When the muscles of the back and the entire body don't have to tense up in order to resist the downward pull of gravity and the spine is aligned against that pull, then the muscles can relax. When this posture is achieved, mental states conducive to meditation are naturally activated—the mind is void of tension and becomes alert. A correlation between body and mind is assumed here. Postures that are tense, compacted, and enclosed evoke mental states that are similarly described. Postures that are aligned, balanced, and expansive trigger similar states of mind.

Although most Asian meditators sit crossed-legged on the floor due to long-standing cultural custom, few meditation teachers see that as a rigid requirement. Whether practitioners sit on the floor, on a cushion, or on a chair, so long as the alignment of the spine frees the easy movement of breathing and allows muscles to relax, the posture is well suited for meditative practice. Relaxation is the crucial requirement. If muscles are flexed in order to hold the body upright, insufficient energy remains for the crucial tasks of mental concentration and spiritual cultivation. Certainly not all meditation exercises seek to relax the mind; the stereotype of Buddhist meditators as always calm and at ease is largely false. Many meditations in fact require energy and mental discipline rather than relaxation. But no matter which mental exercises are in effect, bodily relaxation is always the ideal. When tension and rigidity exist in the body, mental awareness and acuity are diminished.

Meditators are instructed to maintain their balanced posture and to hold still—but not entirely. One of the most important Buddhist tenets is that everything is impermanent and therefore moving. The cycles and movements of breathing attune meditators to the inner movement and processes of the body. Stillness may be all that can be seen from the outside, but whatever inner stillness is experienced is set in a context of the subtle sense of everything in motion.

Although meditation can be practiced outside of formal routines and in the midst of everyday situations, Buddhists claim that taking time out from the activities of life to go into a formal sitting posture is the best way to become fully aware of the most fundamental human processes: the rise and fall of breathing, the emergence and disappearance of multiple bodily sensations, the true character of our current emotions, thoughts, and mental states. Only by temporarily pulling back from ordinary activities do these patterns of life come to consciousness; they are otherwise unknown to us. Nevertheless, meditation is not limited to what happens in formal seated postures. The point is to learn to be present and awake, to use respiratory processes as a concrete connection to the present moment, and to cultivate ease, well-being, and freedom in all postures at all times.

4.8. Is prayer an important practice in Buddhism?

Prayer was not among the primary practices of early Buddhism. The practice of prayer doesn't warrant mention in the three areas of practice in Theravada Buddhism (morality, concentration, wisdom), and it doesn't appear in the Eightfold Path outlined by the Buddha. Because Buddhism in its origins and in the mainstream of tradition as exemplified in its canon of sacred texts is nontheistic—that is, not centered on a deity—the practice of prayer did not have a natural foothold.

By the time a well-developed monotheistic culture emerged in the early centuries of the Common Era, Buddhism was already sufficiently established that it could absorb some influences from this new religious development without altering its basic nontheistic religious structure. The central theistic element of full devotion and submission to a singular deity would appear in some cultural pockets of the tradition without ever bringing about a fundamental transformation in the overall orientation of Buddhism.

If we expand the question beyond prayer to encompass a wider range of devotional practices as gestures of faith, many more Buddhist practices would come into view. The recitation of the Three Jewels, taking refuge in the Buddha, the dharma, and the sangha, shows this devotional element clearly. Taking refuge in the Buddha is something like a vow of faith, and Buddhists in a variety of different traditions recommend these gestures of faith as one preliminary form of calming meditation. Thus, prior to entering into concentration exercises Buddhists have frequently chanted expressions of devotion to the Buddha. This is common among many forms of Buddhism today. Devotional expressions are thought to open the mind of the meditator and to deepen meditative resolve.

Because Mahayana Buddhism emerged as theistic influences were being absorbed by all religions, it was natural that some of these religious elements would also appear in the new Buddhist sutras. In an effort to clarify these new tendencies

Mahayana teachings described three distinct ways to understand who or what the Buddha was, including the possibility of encountering the Buddha in religious visions. This led to a greater role for devotional practices, some of which were similar to prayer.

While important and influential, these theistic elements of practice remained subordinate to other forms of meditation. Because images of deities were always vulnerable to becoming objects of clinging and attachment, they remained under some degree of suspicion. Even as the devotional traditions of Buddhism evolved in later centuries, as in East Asian Pure Land Buddhism, prayer continued to be understood as a devotional meditation on mental images of the Buddha. This kind of prayer as meditation has thrived in Tibet and East Asia. Sharp criticism of prayerful piety has been rare in Buddhist history. More prominent is the sense that Buddhism is comprehensive enough to encompass a wide range of religious styles, including a substantial range of possible relationships between individual Buddhists and the Buddha.

4.9. What practices of moral self-cultivation play a significant role in Buddhism?

As we have seen previously, moral self-cultivation is one of the central components of Buddhist meditation. Buddhists concluded early on that morality is fundamental to a fully awakened life, that human beings are capable of undergoing significant transformation in the moral sphere, and that meditation is the best way to accomplish that.

There are two dimensions of this kind of self-cultivation. One is learning restraint strong enough to resist the pull of negative inclinations such as greed and hatred. The other is learning how to engage in morally positive acts of kindness and generosity. Wherever people are able to reshape their motivations from unwholesome, poisonous desires to un-self-centered inclination, liberating actions naturally follow. This shift in what motivates a person was thought to be enabled by rigorous training that could be accomplished through meditative repetition.

The first five Buddhist precepts have traditionally been the starting point for this training for monastics and the laity. They are restraint from harming living beings, taking what has not been given, sexual misconduct, false speech, and taking intoxicants that lead to negative motivation. (There are another five for monks and nuns.) Rather than simply holding to these rules, Buddhists are taught to identify the troublesome motives that lead to negative behavior and then use meditation to expose and undermine those desires. By repeatedly dwelling on positive motivations and practicing mindful clarity about how those motivations often slip into their opposites, one lays the foundations to deflate one set of powerful motives and to shift that energy into morally positive channels. When the motivations generating our actions change, so do the actions. But all of this change in motivation is thought to take place in meditative training, outside of the sphere of actual actions.

A Buddhist might, for example, become aware of greed as a constantly recurring motive in his or her choices and actions, and following the Buddhist teachings aim to stop imbibing that particular poison (greed being one of the three poisons) since every time we act with greed we sip a little more of that poison and push ourselves further into self-imposed suffering. This Buddhist would seek to become mindful and sensitive to the physical and mental feelings that invariably arise along with greedy motives. Becoming skilled at identifying those concrete feelings allows him or her to know when a moment of concern has arisen. The meditator would delve further into the link between repeated acts of greed and the guilt and suffering that invariably follow.

Understanding this link with clarity might then motivate the meditator to adopt traditional Buddhist meditations on the opposite of greed—on generosity, kindness, and concern for the welfare of others. Or this person might simply construct personal versions of those same exercises by imagining particular people in his or her life for whom imagined acts of generosity and gratitude would be reenacted in the mind, over and over. This mental training is meant to undermine unwholesome motivations and to replace those with positive, skillful motives that have been freely chosen rather than imposed. Over time, Buddhists believe, change will inevitably occur, with the degree and speed of success depending on the sincerity and frequency of the meditation practice.

Similarly, Buddhists might become aware of character traits that stand in the way of wise and compassionate living. Resentment might be traced back to unwholesome modes of self-understanding and to deluded ways of understanding relations between oneself and others. Or moments of intense anger and hatred might be symptoms of one's inner constitution that could be remedied by introspective analysis and meditative reconstruction. All of this is made possible by an image of human ideals that is contained in the Buddhist concept of enlightenment.

Buddhists inherit from the tradition images of what a truly awakened human life might be, and by contemplating those images they aspire to uproot the self-destructive dimensions of their lives in favor of enlightened motivations based on models of human excellence. For many Buddhists, this is called the *thought of enlightenment* or the *mind of awakening* or the *aspiration to awakening*. This deepest source of aspiration offers images of what is possible in human life. Meditations in the sphere of ethics are an essential part of Buddhist practice.

4.10. Are there recognizable stages along the path of Buddhist practice?

There is some difference of opinion on this question within Buddhism. For some the answer is clearly yes, and several

Buddhist texts outline the steps through which Buddhist practitioners progress from beginning to end if they have the discipline. Others, however, are reluctant to generalize to this extent and resist the imposition of standard stages that are applicable to everyone. From their perspective, differences in circumstances, differences in points of departure, in opportunities available, in personal temperaments, orientations, and capacities (and now differences of gender, sexuality, ethnicity, language, cultural background, etc.) render any universal stage theory dubious. Acknowledging at the outset that some Buddhists pay little attention to formal stages of progression, here are some of the most important ways that Buddhists have tried to understand the primary signposts along their path of practice.

Early Buddhist sutras outline several stages along the path toward nirvana. The most widely known of these distinguishes four relatively advanced stages. When practitioners get an initial glimpse of nirvana while still having their vision clouded by several of the defilements, they become *stream-winners*, meaning that they have fully entered the stream of consciousness aimed at nirvana. A stream-winner was thought to face no more than seven rebirths before achieving enlightenment. Stream-winners continue their practices of meditation, overcoming several more of the Ten Fetters.

When two more of the fetters, sensual desire and ill will, are virtually eliminated, meditators become *once-returners*. Such a person will enter the human realm just one more time and will pursue the disciplines of meditation at such advanced levels that progress along the path is rapid. At the end of that life of practice, meditators become *never-returners*, who one by one destroy the remaining fetters that hold them back from nirvana. With full success in that endeavor, the meditator becomes an *arhat*, someone who has finally completed the path of purification, thus entering the state of nirvana while still living.

Similar stages along the path are articulated with special reference to the practice of meditation. There are efforts to articulate the stages of calming meditation and others for insight meditation. Two versions of the stages of insight meditation are the early Buddhist Seven Purifications and the Five Paths.

Indian Mahayana Buddhists were also motivated to attempt outlines of the structure of the path. Perhaps the most famous of these are presented in the *Sutra of Ten Stages*, which attempts to define the progress through which an aspiring bodhisattva would inevitably travel. In the first stage a bodhisattva experiences profound joy at having entered the path and gotten a partial glimpse of the truth. Second, motives are purified to the point that one is immune to defilements. Third, one begins to radiate a sense of wisdom. Fourth, wisdom overcomes all personal worldly desires. Fifth, meditative powers of deep concentration are perfected. Sixth, wisdom is openly manifest. Seventh, one transcends attachment to Buddhism by going beyond the two vehicles. Eighth, one dwells firmly and imperturbably on the path of the Middle Way. Ninth, abilities to teach the dharma spontaneously are perfected. And tenth, one lives completely for the benefit of all living beings. Like the stages of the stream-winner, these Mahayana Buddhist stages are all situated at a relatively high level and ignore what one might have had to go through to arrive at that initial stage.

Also from a classic Mahayana text, the *Avatamsaka* sutra, there is a compelling literary account of the pilgrimage of a bodhisattva named Sudhana who travels to visit fifty-two different teachers, each one representing a further stage of development and revealing more advanced insight to be gleaned along the path. In this story, we have essentially fifty-two stages from the beginning of the pilgrimage to the consummation of wisdom at the climax.

Other stage theories appear throughout the history of Buddhist thought, but none receives as much attention as these. Contrary instincts within Buddhism place more emphasis on the skills of improvisation that would be needed if human beings were so diverse in temperament and orientation that no single outline of the path would suffice.

4.11. Are there ascetic practices that are important for Buddhists?

Officially, Buddhists do not engage in ascetic practices. Recall that the Buddha himself rejected his own experiments with asceticism, declaring Buddhism to be the Middle Way between the self-indulgence of pleasure-seeking and the self-torture of ascetic practice. Asceticism in most religious contexts is typically grounded in theories of body/mind dualism, a stark division between one's physical being and one's spiritual life. Buddhism explicitly rejects that form of dualism, thereby undermining the grounds for denigrating the body. One of the Buddha's key insights was that a strong, healthy body would be necessary to provide a solid foundation for spiritual life, and this insight has been important throughout the many traditions of Buddhism. The Buddha's rejection of ascetic practice helped legitimize the Middle Way of moderation and good judgment as a check on tendencies to radical self-denial.

Remember, though, that for the Buddha himself such moderation meant sleeping on the open ground without bedding, living without possessions, and eating only what happened to be offered during the morning hours of begging. For us, and for most Buddhists, that's far from moderation. That the precise location of this line between moderate and extreme might shift radically over time and between different kinds of Buddhists is certainly understandable. We know that from the earliest historical records monks tended to be classified into two types. *Town dwellers* lived in proximity to ordinary society, and this tendency in Buddhism quickly developed into monasteries that could comfortably house a few or many monks. Others, however, were *forest dwellers* who lived lives of stern discipline and abstention from all the comforts of civilized life. The ascetic instincts of early Indian religion lived on among these forest-dwelling monks.

We find, then, that an interesting array of ascetic practices does appear in Buddhism, and in certain cases attains full legitimacy, even fame and admiration. Perhaps the best-known example is the monastic practice of fire walking in Sri Lanka and to some extent in Southeast Asia. After a large evening fire has burned down to coals, these are spread out on the ground for thirty feet or so. After immersion in meditative concentration, monks (and sometimes lay people) walk barefoot across the coals, hoping not to be severely injured in the experience. The idea that mind might prevail over matter, that a profound enough state of concentration can shield the body against the burning of skin, seems to imply the resurgence of at least some degree of mind/body dualism. These practices also emphasize mental attributes of faith and courage, in addition to the depth of concentration made possible through meditation.

Tibetan Buddhists also show great admiration for ascetic practices. Milarepa, the great Buddhist yogi of Tibet, was ordered by Marpa, his teacher, to build a house by hand without tools. When the house was completed after an arduous struggle with dirt and stone, Milarepa's teacher had him tear it down and begin again. This went on for years, and the justification given was that Milarepa had accumulated so much bad karma that extreme penance would be required to burn it off. For centuries stories circulated in Tibet of monks covering themselves with water-soaked robes to sit out in near freezing weather deeply absorbed in meditation. They are reputed to be capable of concentrated body control to the point of raising their physical temperature far above the human norm, even to the point of being able to heat and dry their otherwise frozen garb. These stories and others attained great fame even if they were not widely imitated.

Another Tibetan example is the famed pilgrimage to and circumambulation of Mount Kailash, an enormous and starkly beautiful mountain. Many Tibetans attempt this arduous act of ascetic devotion. To circumambulate Kailash on its thirty-two-mile trail in one day, as the customary ideal demands, is extremely difficult given the cold, high elevation, oxygen-depleted air, and rocky terrain. Yet an astonishingly large number of Tibetans—monastic and lay—manage to do it. Even more extraordinary are those who complete this act of devotion not by walking but by making hundreds of thousands of body-length prostrations over four or more weeks of endurance and meditative prayer. In these religious acts the body manages astonishing feats through the added empowerment of deep devotional meditation.

In Japanese Buddhism we find equally strenuous examples of ascetic prowess. On Mount Hiei in central Japan, monks of the Tendai order train themselves in extreme distance running as a form of meditation. Far beyond the well-known difficulty of marathon races, these monks learn to run all day long, focusing on the respiratory processes that are equally fundamental to both meditation and running. In the most extreme version, monks take the challenge of a thousand-mile run that demands a continual jog over many days. In Japanese Zen Buddhism, we find monks who undertake an intensive meditation session of one or two weeks in which they never lie down to sleep. Sitting in meditation posture twenty-four hours a day, they use the psychic extremes of sleep deprivation to push their mental state to a level of crisis where it is hoped that a moment of radical awakening might break through ordinary consciousness.

4.12. What role does ritual play in Buddhist practice?

The short answer to this question is that ritual plays a major role in Buddhist practice, perhaps similar in importance to other highly developed religions. At the outset of modern

Western interest in Buddhism, however, this claim would have been both counterintuitive and unwelcome. Because of the central role of meditation and because Buddhism was not primarily oriented toward a theistic deity, it was assumed that Buddhism would be the exception among religions and that the ritualized tendencies of the other traditions would have been left behind by Buddhists. That assumption has turned out to be false. Furthermore, a contemporary interest in ritual has developed that rejects the previous romantic claim that ritual is an inherently inauthentic form of religion. Buddhist rituals, especially those associated with the practices of mindfulness and meditation, have attracted considerable attention.

Let's begin with the most important early Buddhist rituals, those performed regularly by monks and nuns. If by "ritual" we mean a regularly enacted physical performance of religious significance, then several early Buddhist rituals stand out. First, monks and nuns engaged in rituals of meditation on a daily basis, sometimes for many hours of the day. Scant evidence exists for how this was done, but if later practice is any guide meditation was conducted communally rather that individually. Monks or nuns gathered together to engage in this practice in a prescribed way. Later meditation rituals followed a specific order, including a ritualized beginning and end. Today each type of Buddhism follows its own patterns of meditation ritual, but in every case the pattern of actions is prescribed and followed meticulously, freeing all participants from the demands of decision-making. The prescribed order allows a stress-free entrance into meditative mindfulness that facilitates access to more concentrated states of mind.

The ritual of begging also follows a specific pattern, one that monks, nuns, and lay people can anticipate. Robed monastics enter the village at a set time before noon and stand with begging bowls extended in a precise manner. Words exchanged are largely prescribed too, and the comfortable prearranged routine allows people an opportunity to share in the equanimity of their guests.

Of particular importance because it would occur only once in the life of a monk or nun was the ritual in which monastic participants were ordained and accepted into the order. Full ordination was possible at the age of twenty, and the ritual of admittance required the presence of at least five monks of advanced standing. In the ceremony newly ordained monks recite their responsibility of adherence to the code of discipline, which was devised to promote an ordered and peaceful way of life aimed specifically at awakening.

Following ordination, all monks and nuns take part twice a month in ceremonies attended by all other monks and nuns in the community. Together they recite the prohibitions one by one, asking in each case if anyone has transgressed the rule. Those who have step forth to offer confession before the recitation proceeds to the next rule. The rules are arranged in sequence of severity, beginning with those requiring expulsion from the sangha. Regular recitation of the Buddhist code is meant to foster a full internalization not just of the rules themselves but of the moral sensitivity that the rules cultivate.

Buddhist ritual plays an expanded role in the Tantric traditions of Tibet and East Asia. There ritual practice and meditation practice are virtually identical, and a concentrated, meditative state of mind in ritual participation is of the utmost importance. Initiation of students into full-status practitioners is perhaps most significant. On these occasions the teacher or guru initiates students into the sacred patterns of ritual. The student vows confidence in the guru's guidance and confesses an intention of faithful obedience. The ceremony occurs within a *mandala*, a space set apart from the mundane world by a circular chalk marking, and initiates are told to study and memorize the diagrams drawn within the mandala. The idea here is that religious patterns in the mandala are then spiritualized by being imprinted in the practitioner's mind. The guru teaches a *mantra*, a brief verse or phrase that is thought to invoke the deepest dimension of mind whenever recited. Sacred *mudras*, symbolic gestures, are taught that correspond to the sounds of

the chanted mantra. Tantric ritual thus demands full engagement of the student's body, speech, and mind and aims at an
awakening in each sphere.

Specific rituals and the details of their performance vary
significantly from one Buddhist culture to another and over
historical time. Some are followed daily, some weekly or
monthly, and others mark the calendar year. Annual rituals
include New Year celebrations and ritual remembrance of
the Buddha's birthday and enlightenment. There are rituals
specific to founders of each sect, those honoring famous
predecessors, and others that offer consecration of the nation
and its leadership.

Submission to specific ritual action is thought to foster a
sense of humility and selflessness in participants. Practiced in
a meditative mindset, ritual is meant to help cultivate mindfulness, self-control, and wisdom. Some Buddhist rituals cul-
minate in a ritualized transfer of merit to others that aims
to inculcate the sensitivities of empathy and compassion.
Practitioners recite words that offer to others any positive
merit that might be earned by the performance of the ritual,
either relatives or the needy, or simply to all sentient beings.
Participants end by rejoicing in the possibility of wholesome
acts performed in the spirit of generosity without dwelling on
benefit to themselves.

4.13. How do scripture and reading function in Buddhist practice?

In early Buddhist cultures the teachings were most often
disseminated by word of mouth. Hearing the dharma, spoken
perhaps by a wandering monk or nun and later by priests in
a temple, was the most common conversion mechanism, the
way Buddhist ideas and aspirations entered people's minds
and character. Literacy was the purview of the elite, as in
other cultures, and Buddhist monasteries were often the most

important venue for teaching and learning the arts of reading and writing.

Once the sutras and other important texts were written, reading the dharma in a meditative environment became a more and more frequent practice in all Buddhist cultures. Sermons and talks of various kinds continued to be essential aspects of the culture of Buddhism, especially for the many people who could not read. But as Buddhist cultures absorbed the benefits of literacy to greater and greater degrees, reading as a medium of religious inspiration increased.

Throughout Asia, reading the sacred texts of Buddhism came to be considered a particularly meritorious practice. Beyond the learning and internalization of ideas that derive from patient reading, many Buddhists have believed that the simple act of reading the dharma is a potent source of additional karmic merit. This has on occasion led to magical conceptions of the benefits of reading and, based on that idea, abuses of the practice. Some Buddhists believed that the mere mechanics of running your eyes over the sutras' words—without the added difficulty of trying to understand them—was sufficient to accumulate merit. In a few locations, sutra sentences or phrases were placed inside prayer wheels so that the mechanical effort of spinning the wheel would maximize merit for the practitioner. In these cases, the mental separation of the act itself from the meditative engagement with it as a form of practice gave rise to criticisms from other Buddhists.

Other criticisms of reading as a form of practice in Buddhism appeared over time. In Chan or Zen, Buddhist texts were ridiculed as "dung clods" or "worthless dust," and stories circulated about radical Zen masters who irreverently burned the sutras or ripped them to shreds. But this critique focused primarily on the quality of the practice of reading, on how or why it was being done. Reading for scholarly or merely academic purposes was frequently subjected to ridicule. Seeking information about the dharma was contrasted with the authentic effort to fully embody the dharma in one's life. Even after these powerful criticisms, reading continued to be practiced, of course; in fact it grew in importance. But how and why this reading was practiced became a regular topic of debate and critique.

One reading practice that has flourished in many Buddhist cultures is chanting the sutras. Whether monks or nuns in a monastery or large gatherings of lay people in a temple, reading or reciting a sutra out loud and in unison was considered an important type of meditation, one that gathered many minds into a unified act of contemplation. In all of these forms, reading has been a widely practiced and insufficiently appreciated form of Buddhist practice for many centuries. Its relation to meditation as a whole is rarely considered.

4.14. Are artistic images of the Buddha important in settings of Buddhist practice?

It is doubtful that painted or sculpted representations of the Buddha existed in the early centuries of Buddhism because the tradition was firmly opposed to such representations. Thus we have no idea what the Buddha looked like, nor are there written descriptions of his appearance traceable to this period.

Symbolic representations of the Buddha and of Buddhism appeared in burial mounds (*stupas*) that were thought to have contained relic traces of the Buddha—a bone, a tooth, or a fragment of one of his few possessions. Over time these became focal points of devotional practice such as meditative circumambulation. The best known of these stupas were located at sites where important events in the life of the Buddha had occurred: Lumbini grove, where he was born; Bodh Gaya, where he was awakened; the deer park near Varanasi where he first taught; and the site of his death. Monks, nuns, and lay people have frequently traveled to these places to engage in devotional meditation.

Other symbols of Buddhism during the early period were the bodhi tree, the wheel, and the footprint. Meditating in the presence of these sacred images was considered the most efficacious preliminary practice, the best way to generate the resolve to engage in a dedicated life of contemplative inquiry.

By the first century of the Common Era, however, the prohibition on direct representation of the Buddha seems to have eased. Perhaps with the rise of theistic religions throughout India, including the development of devotional Buddhism, and perhaps with the Mahayana interest in broad appeal to people of all kinds, Buddhist images began to appear in the monasteries of northern India.

Early images of the Buddha in a Hellenistic sculpted style were created in the Gandhara region of northern India, where multiple cultural influences converged. Depictions of the Buddha in particular moments in his life, in specific postures, or mudras, and eventually in the serene transcendental pose of perfection that became most prominent, were employed more and more often in settings of Buddhist practice. Devotional chants as well as offerings of flowers and incense became standard Buddhist practices at these sites. These images in a range of variations and the practices associated with them spread quickly through all Buddhist cultures and remain today one of the primary settings for the practice of Buddhism.

4.15. Do sacred sites and pilgrimages have a function in Buddhist practice?

Pilgrimage to sacred sites has long been an important practice among Buddhists, especially lay practitioners. An early sutra even depicts the Buddha himself commending this practice. In the early centuries of Buddhism, four sites in India stood out as the most efficacious pilgrimages to commemorate the Buddha. The first of these is Lumbini, the grove of trees in which Gautama was born, now near the Nepalese-Indian border. This site flourished for centuries as a place of devotion and meditation but fell into disrepair as Buddhism died out in

India. It was rediscovered by archaeologists a little over a century ago and is now quickly becoming a favorite location for Buddhist pilgrimage.

The second of four major pilgrimages focused on the life of the Buddha is Bodh Gaya, the site where Gautama experienced enlightenment under the Bodhi Tree. There pilgrims circumambulate the enormous Great Enlightenment Temple (Mahabodhi), a giant stupa reputed to house relics of the Buddha. Many other temples have been added, often sponsored by Buddhist groups from other countries, giving pilgrims from those countries a stake in the sacred location. Extensive commercial development there and at the other sacred sites, although off-putting to some, has not slowed the volume of pilgrims.

The third location is Sarnath, the deer park outside current Varanasi, already a sacred place at that time, where the newly enlightened Buddha first taught the dharma to his formerly ascetic friends. Finally, there is Kushinagar, the location of the Buddha's death. Archaeological evidence shows the remains of several monasteries and temples that clearly thrived at this site for centuries.

These four pilgrimage sites were the most important for lay Buddhists in the early centuries of the tradition. Monks and nuns were involved as well, but less as pilgrims than as residents in monasteries that were constructed on these sacred sites and as overseers of the temples that travelers visited. Pilgrims came to engage in devotional meditations, recollecting various phases in the life of the Buddha. They made offerings of flowers, candles, and incense; listened to talks by monks and nuns; circumambulated the sacred site; and made donations of money to support the temples. No doubt occasional festivals attracted pilgrims at specific times during the year.

We have moving accounts of these sites from Chinese pilgrims who dared make the dangerous overland trek to India in the early centuries of the Common Era. They report visiting sacred relics of the Buddha. But when Buddhism fell into steep decline centuries later, these sites also failed, some of their buildings simply yielding to time and weather, while others were actively destroyed by invading forces establishing non-Buddhist rule in India.

4.16. Is art or music employed in Buddhist practice?

Buddhist temples, whether rural or urban, are strikingly beautiful sites designed to encourage and deepen religious practice. But there is tremendous cultural variation among them. Consider first a temple in Theravada Buddhist Thailand. Tranquil meditation gardens surround temples (*wats*), often with several distinctive stupa structures. Interiors of prominent temples are sumptuous displays of gold: statues of the Buddha covered in gold leaf, ritual instruments of pure gold, sometimes against a background of perhaps even more gold paint.

Now imagine a Tibetan temple profusely colored inside and out. The brightest blues, yellows, reds, and greens are painted in intricate patterns, both abstract design and narrative depictions of important Tibetan lamas. Mandala paintings outlined in equally colorful silk brocade adorn the walls, all illuminated by numerous candles or butter lamps flickering for added effect. The temple's natural backdrop is of course profoundly colorless. Located at high elevation above the tree line, where little vegetation and very few flowers hide the sand and rock, the temple competes only with the sky to bring to life the visual palette of illuminating color.

For sheer contrast, enter a Japanese Zen temple. It is not colorless but is restricted in its color palate to gardens of plant green and rock gray. The wooden exterior and interior walls are unpainted; the floors of polished dark wood or tatami rice mats are the setting for the display of very few art objects, the architecture and gardens being the aesthetic focus. Paintings sparsely placed on the walls typically feature black ink on white rice paper, either a simple painted image or calligraphy or both woven together on one scroll. There might be a small altar with a wooden Buddha or bodhisattva image, but only if it avoids ostentation and bright colors.

In each of these very diverse temple settings local aesthetic sensibilities and art traditions step forward to adorn Buddhism in a particular native way. In each case, the architecture—of buildings, entrances, and gardens—attracts attention and establishes an atmosphere conducive to the particular kinds of practice that occur there, whether meditation, teachings, devotion, or other forms of practice.

If there is an aspect of Buddhist culture that is less fully developed than Buddhism's 2,500-year history might lead us to expect, it would be music. One explanation for this is that in India, the country of Buddhism's origins, the rich and sophisticated classical tradition of music came to fruition long after Buddhism had declined and disappeared there. The same might be the case in the other monumental Buddhist culture, China, which by 1300 had lost its appetite for the creative edge of Buddhism, drawing instead on native Confucian traditions. As a result, perhaps, the finest examples of Buddhist music appear on the periphery of these massive cultures, most notably in Tibet and Japan, where instrumental music is played in temple settings. Tibetan drums and horns lend a festival atmosphere to Buddhist gatherings, and in Zen the solo bamboo flute conjures moods of mystery and depth.

But by far the most important musical dimension of Buddhist practice is chanting, a religious recitation in musical form, often without instrumental accompaniment aside from percussion. Both lay and monastic Buddhists frequently engage in chanting, and we can find it in virtually all types of Buddhism. Its official role is to prepare the practitioners' minds for meditation. In many settings chanting *is* meditation, and its function is to clear, concentrate, and focus the mind. Chanting also accompanies many forms of ritual in Buddhism. One early sutra warns Buddhists about attachment to chanting, but the practice has thrived in spite of that warning.

In the Tantric tradition, chanting precedes all ritual and is an essential element in that ritual. Ritual may be dedicated to or focused on a particular Buddhist deity or concept, and in these cases chanting functions to settle the mind directly on the object of the dedication. The most common and famous Tibetan chant is *OM Mani Padme Hum*, an homage to the Bodhisattva of Compassion. Tibetan monks are also famous for having perfected the art of throat chanting, a voice technique that allows musical chords to emerge from a single chanter.

In East Asia, Pure Land Buddhists chant the *nembutsu* as frequently as they can—*Namu Amida Butsu*, an homage to Amida Buddha—in temple rituals and also individually in the midst of daily life, either outwardly as song or inwardly as silent meditation. Other Mahayana Buddhists, especially Shingon and Zen, chant the *Perfection of Wisdom* sutras, focusing on the brief *Heart* sutra and occasionally on the longer *Diamond* sutra. These chants are rhythmic monotone meditations on the principal theme of these sutras, the interconnected emptiness of all things. And finally, Nichiren Buddhists in Japan and now elsewhere are famous for a chant generated by the allure of the *Lotus* sutra, *Nam Myoho Renge Kyo*.

4.17. What role do priests, gurus, or other religious professionals play for Buddhist practitioners?

As we have seen, Buddhism began not as a religion encompassing the entire society but as an extraordinary spiritual option that certain individuals found attractive. The quest for enlightenment meant an awakening from the pull of ordinary social, political, and economic life, a life of renunciation, abstinence, and discipline that only select individuals pursued. Yet as monastic Buddhism grew, its dependence on and contribution to the society as a whole expanded as well. Both political leaders and ordinary citizens began to see the presence of Buddhist monks and nuns in their area as a substantial benefit for everyone. Buddhist monastics strove to make themselves worthy of the material support that ordinary working people provided. Monks and nuns attempted to model a moral life that people would respect and admire. As a result, they were often placed in the role of village teachers. Town-dwelling monastics were of particular importance; the functions they performed in village and city life evolved as needs and opportunities arose.

Members of the sangha made themselves available to help fulfill the needs of others. When a lay person began a new enterprise, built a new house, held a wedding, or died, such occasions were opportunities for monks and nuns to serve the society. Members of the Buddhist sangha would attend special occasions and celebrations of these kinds, often to chant blessings or to consecrate the event. Monastics did not preside officially over the events and were therefore not acting in a role that we might regard as priestly. But their presence established bonds that over time would place Buddhists in that priestly role.

In Thailand and much of Southeast Asia, monks adopted a variety of priestly roles. As teachers, they taught in the spirit of the dharma, teaching the dharma directly along with all other educational curricula, from literacy to math. Ceremonies of all kinds—but especially funerals—invariably require the presence and oversight of monks. Monks frequently counsel local lay Buddhists, serve as arbiters in disputes, and are regarded as the voice of wisdom in many similar settings.

In Tibetan Buddhism the role of the lama is of great importance. Lamas are high priests who are gurus or teachers of the dharma and much more. They conduct ceremonies of many kinds and oversee the maintenance of temples and religious monuments. They tend to the sick, settle disputes, read omens, make predictions, and offer formal blessings for new homes, places of work, schools, and other institutions. In Tibet celibacy is not required of all lamas, and it is very often the case that village lamas are married and have families.

Tibet's Tantric traditions place great importance on the personal relations between an aspiring Buddhist and his or her guru. Above the lamas are higher level teachers, Rinpoches, who are believed to be fully awakened bodhisattvas. Important lamas and all Buddhists at the level of Rinpoche offer initiations into more elevated dimensions of the Buddhist teachings that are not available to or suitable for everyone. The full depth of enlightenment is open to aspirants through the lamas' instruction, making their participation in the lives of both monks and lay people of central importance.

In Japan, a similar role is played by Zen masters and Vajrayana (Shingon) priests. These leaders are esteemed for the depth of their spiritual attainment and aspire to pass this state of mind on to others. As in Tibetan Buddhism, some Japanese monks serve the full spectrum of priestly roles. They conduct a variety of ceremonies, especially funerals, offer counseling and guidance, and attend to as many of the needs of lay people as possible. Here too, if they have not taken a vow of celibacy, Buddhist priests can marry, have children, and participate in society in a variety of roles.

4.18. How is Tantric practice distinct from earlier forms of Buddhist practice?

Although all forms of Buddhism view practice as the essence of the tradition, few are as explicit about this focus as the Tantric or Vajrayana tradition. This tradition developed in later Indian Buddhism and has been adopted in Tibet and Mongolia, and to a lesser extent in China, Korea, and Japan. As several great Tibetan Buddhists have claimed, the only substantial distinction between Mahayana Buddhism and Vajrayana Buddhism is the dimension of practice, in which the Vajrayana is considered to be a more direct, faster path to the ultimate goal of fully awakened Buddhahood.

Tantric Buddhists affirm the key Mahayana teachings of the emptiness or impermanence and contingency of all aspects of reality, the path of the bodhisattva who seeks enlightenment not just on his or her own behalf but on behalf of all sentient beings, and the rejection of the sacred/profane divide based on the realization that nirvana is the ordinary world of samsara properly experienced. Like later Mahayana Buddhists, Tantric Buddhists affirm the inner presence of enlightenment, the seed of Buddhahood already present within all beings. They also affirm the necessity of skillful means to bring human beings to this profound realization since so much of ordinary human experience functions to block or obscure deeper awareness of our world.

The preliminary practices commonly employed in the Vajrayana include virtually all elements of earlier forms of Buddhism. Calming (*samatha*) and insight (*vipassana*) meditation, meditative recitation of the Three Jewels—"taking refuge in the Buddha, the dharma, and the sangha"—are essential points of departure. Tantric Buddhists meditate in order to arouse *bodhicitta*, the bodhisattva's aspiration to pursue awakening on behalf of all beings. Confession as practiced in earlier Buddhism is important. In this ritual, participants acknowledge their own negative actions and vow to actively reverse those destructive patterns. Full prostrations are commonly practiced in Tantric Buddhism as a bodily means of bringing repentance to mind.

Having undertaken these preliminary practices, students are positioned to receive the distinctive skillful means of the Vajrayana. This tradition insists on *esoteric transmission*, meaning that the teachings are communicated only personally from the teacher or guru directly to the student rather than being available for anyone at any time. The rationale for this secrecy is that Vajrayana teachings are gradually disclosed through a sequence of stages only when individual students are in a mental and spiritual position to understand and benefit from them. Prior to that readiness, it is thought that these teachings would only confuse and undermine the good intentions of the student. A personal, practical relationship between the teacher and the student is therefore vital since what the teacher has to communicate can't be disseminated in written form. Student and teacher must develop trust for this kind of teaching to be effective. In order to initiate disciples into increasingly complex levels of insight gurus must understand each student's particular orientation and capacities very well. Some practices involve the student visualizing the teacher as the embodiment of the Buddhahood that the student seeks.

Because the world of nirvana *is* the world of samsara, Tantric practices employ elements of the ordinary world in their quest for awakening. Foremost among these are mandalas, mantras, and mudras. Mandalas are symbolic, circular diagrams of reality. They operate on several levels. Symbolic representations of awakened Buddhas and bodhisattvas surround the diagram to serve as objects of meditation on the qualities of enlightened comportment. These figures also represent a map of human psychological reality, and the juxtaposition of one level on another allows meditative insight into the relations between them. Meditating on the mandala is thought to enable the practitioner to see his or her own awakened potential.

Mantras are verbal invocations addressed both to awakened Buddhas and bodhisattvas and to one's own inner nature—the Buddha nature. Practitioners repeatedly intone mantras as a physical, bodily form of meditation. Mudras are body movements concentrated in the hands, thought to invoke the presence within the person of these enlightened qualities of character. Tantric ritual employs these three techniques simultaneously as its distinct meditative style.

One distinctive Tantric practice that employs these elements is called *deity yoga*, in which the practitioner evokes the awakened Buddhas and bodhisattvas represented in a mandala diagram. Most important among these is the practitioner's own personal deity, a Buddha image or bodhisattva figure chosen by practitioners in consultation with their teacher as the image most suitable to bring them to direct experiential insight. The student visualizes this image to absorb its characteristics while avoiding attachment. This means that the student dwells upon the concrete form of the image while simultaneously realizing its emptiness, that is, its contingency, impermanence, and limitations. The image personifies practitioners' own awakened potential as they cultivate the mental ability to actualize it. Because these images of enlightened perfection demonstrate one's own limitations and afflictions, the process of meditating through them is thought to require enormous concentration, discipline, and the guidance of a guru.

The Vajrayana is also well known for practices that use the most problematic dimensions of the ordinary world as the focal point for spiritual practice. Social taboos can provide strong catalysts for the emergence of awakening. Sexual yoga is one such practice, in which the early Buddhist prohibition and the subsequent mental knots of repression surrounding sexuality become the center of meditative focus. Intentional violations of dietary taboos or social taboos like the Indian caste system function to create a level of turbulence in the mind that has the potential to push someone through to a deeper level of insight and a new way of relating to the prohibitions. These practices are notorious because they purposefully transgress upon the most sensitive subjects. Only certain Vajrayana teachers take the risks entailed in these practices, and widespread acceptance of them has never been achieved.

4.19. How has Zen practice developed in its own distinct way?

To take just one more example of a highly evolved and specialized style of Buddhist practice, it is instructive to look at Zen Buddhism. Chan, or Zen, originated as a potent critique of the scholarly and intellectually sophisticated forms of Buddhism that had dominated China for several centuries. Zen focused on direct paths to awakening with meditation the essential element along that path. The tradition distinguished itself by locating monasteries in rural areas, by finding financial support from sources other than government, and by developing the mystique of enlightened masters who focused intently on meditative practice and achievement while downplaying the earlier discipline of mastering the Buddhist sutras that had linked the Chinese tradition so firmly to earlier Indian sources. Practice was primary. Although Zen history is long and diverse, the following forms of practice are widespread:

- All acts are practice. Zen practice begins with the instruction to regard everything you do as engagement in spiritual practice on a par with sitting on a meditation cushion. This is an effort to break through the dichotomy between spiritual practice and all other practices; everything done in Zen is to be performed in a meditative state of mind. As in other traditions of Buddhist meditation, this begins with observing the breath. Breathing is what we do while also engaged in everything else we do, so Zen teachers instruct practitioners to focus there, to simply observe the respiratory process as the diaphragm expands and contracts to keep the flow of air moving through the body. To maintain that awareness while gardening, cooking, or bathing makes all acts practice.
- Observe the mind. Like earlier Indian Buddhist meditators, Zen students are taught to maintain awareness of the stream of consciousness as thoughts, feelings, and intentions come and go. The task is simply to sit there, or just be there and watch, keeping enough distance from the flow of mental states in order to refrain from attaching oneself to any of them. No judgment, no purpose, no plan is imposed. When asked why, some Zen adepts say "We're just sitting!" The effort is simply to witness what's there without having one's intention captured by any element of the rapidly moving drama.
- Rituals of intensive meditation (*sesshin*). Periodically Zen teachers break the routines of ordinary temple life to guide students through several days or up to two weeks in which formal sitting meditation is practiced as much

as twelve to fourteen hours per day, and on occasion even more. Intensive meditations—what in contemporary Buddhism are often called "retreats"—are regarded as the setting best suited to experiences of awakening.

- Koan inquiry. Koan cases are brief riddles thought to embody enlightened teachings or actions by past Zen masters and on that basis are used as objects of meditation. At a certain stage of advancement, Zen masters assign a particular koan case to students with the intention that they will pursue insight from the koan until they are able to provide a response that is satisfactory to the master. As in Vajrayana practice, the teacher-student relationship is crucial in Zen, especially in the context of koan practice.

- Individual meetings with the Zen master. In the midst of an intensive meditation session, but at other times as well, students one by one leave the meditation hall to consult with their teachers in private. Highly formal and ritualized, the occasion is one of considerable mental tension since the master examines the students' state of mind through question and answer. In all cases where koans have been assigned, *that* becomes the sole focus of discussion, and students are expected to present a response to the koan puzzle. This response is not an answer in the typical sense of that word, but rather a demonstration of insight.

- Labor as practice. Early in the history of Chan Buddhism, a story began to circulate that an elderly abbot, Baizhang, had refused to eat because, out of compassion for his fragility, younger monks had hidden his garden tools, thus preventing him from engaging in manual labor along with them. The abbot's response became a defining slogan in Zen: "A day without labor is a day without food." Although it had already been customary for Zen monks to engage in such labor, as the tradition evolved, stories like this one helped to make work an important part of Zen religious practice. After morning meditation, all monks have a work assignment, and the challenge to each of them is to take the concentrated state of mind-fulness that they had cultivated in the meditation hall and bring it out into the world of ordinary activity. If, they reasoned, the Zen state of mind wasn't directly applicable to the rest of life, what would be the point of cultivating it?

• Liturgy and chanting practice. In virtually all Zen contexts, prior to engagement in seated meditation a simple ritual of devotional commitment and chanting occurs. The liturgy for these rituals is designed to build a sense of dedication to the meditative task at hand. Brief sutras, most notably the *Heart* sutra, are chanted in unison, as are chants of commemorative gratitude for the work of Zen founders and key figures whose inspiration has made current participation possible.

• Zen dharma talks. Although the tradition was founded on a slogan of nonreliance on language and texts, regular sermons by leading masters are a basic part of Zen practice. Such talks are often riddled with the kind of paradoxical and spirited language that is often found in the classic stories of past Zen masters. Getting the point of the talk and making meditative use of it are important elements in Zen practice. Although silence pervades the atmosphere of a Zen temple, when words are spoken they take on a significance that goes to the heart of Zen practice.

4.20. Do Buddhists try to win converts?

Aggressive proselytizing has been discouraged since the beginning of Buddhism. The traditional rule is that Buddhists are to teach or discuss the dharma with non-Buddhists only when the non-Buddhists have requested it. Indeed, in a couple of traditions, Buddhists decline to teach until asked three times. The basic rules of the Buddhist order prohibit teaching the dharma to anyone who appears to be uninterested or disrespectful. Although there have been a couple of notorious violations of this rule about proselytizing, they are surprisingly few given that Buddhism is the world's first universal religion—that is, a religion not grounded in ethnic, racial, linguistic, or national identity. Buddhists clearly believed that the dharma was a universal remedy for the tragic preponderance of human suffering and that anyone who received the gift of the dharma would be awakened from the self-imposed trauma of ordinary life.

Early accounts of the Buddha's enlightenment portray him as unsure about whether the dharma was teachable and about whether he should dedicate his life to the task of teaching. The early biographies tell us that for weeks he sat in the shade of the Bodhi Tree to ponder these questions. Clearly his answer was that he would teach, indeed that he must teach in order to make this liberating possibility available to anyone whose karmic position in life led them to be interested. Early monks, following in the footsteps of the Buddha, did just that as well. They wandered the Indian countryside from village to village, teaching when asked to do so.

The bodhisattva vow, a formal or informal vow to practice the disciplines of Buddhism not simply on behalf of one's own enlightenment but for everyone, is an important part of Mahayana Buddhism. This meant that aspiring Mahayana Buddhists sought the skills of selfless, wise teaching capable of extending the dharma to people of very different backgrounds, capacities, interests, and sensibilities. One of the essential skills was understanding when, how, and whether to teach, knowing that the Buddhist path requires a commitment of discipline and not just a conversion of beliefs. They also realized that inner serenity and humility were crucial for a successful teacher and that rigid attachment to one's own beliefs was a clear sign of delusion, if not greed. A Zen saying claims that if you stare at the finger pointing to the moon you will never see the moon. Buddhist teachings and practice point to awakening but should never be grasped and coveted as though they are the goal itself. As the Mahayana sutras claim, all things are contingent—empty of absolute status—the dharma included.

When the Dalai Lama presents open lectures, frequently to more non-Buddhists than Buddhists, he often tells the audience that there is no need to convert to Buddhism. His advice is to take advantage of Buddhism whenever that is helpful but to focus instead on the wisdom available in whatever tradition has come to be their own.

5

CONTEMPORARY
GLOBAL BUDDHISM

5.1. Is Buddhism a religion, and if so in what sense?

This question has perplexed Westerners ever since their first encounters with Buddhism in the eighteenth century. Early missionaries, merchants, and government officials living in Asia wrote home in confusion. On the surface, Buddhism certainly seemed religious. There were temples, monks and nuns, devout practitioners performing rituals—all clear signs of religion. But one crucial element seemed to be missing or at least badly misplaced: God. The original scriptures never even mention a supreme deity or creator, and although there are occasional references to various minor deities, these seem to be largely beside the point of Buddhism. Without God, is Buddhism still a religion?

My tactic here is to summarize arguments for the three leading positions on this question, and let the reader decide: (1) No, Buddhism is not a religion; (2) Yes, of course it is; and (3) The question itself is misleading.

Proponents of the No position are many. They argue that Buddhism is a way of life, a philosophy, a psychology, a set of ethical and meditative practices aimed at living an enlightened life, or even personal techniques to relieve anxiety and suffering in life, and all of these can be supported by substantial evidence. They claim that the teachings of the Buddha allow no room for the God of creation, that Buddhist morality doesn't require divine oversight, and that worship isn't among the many practices that the Buddha taught. They point out that neither belief nor dogma is required, that the Buddha clearly encouraged personal investigation and inquiry, and that practices for overcoming human delusion and suffering are the overwhelming focus of Buddhist attention. Although they admit an element of transcendence in Buddhism, what is transcended are the limitations of our own egos, our narrow, self-interested perspective, our emotional clinging, and our personal illusions. The fact that Buddhism is oriented in these ways, they claim, would qualify Buddhism as a way of life or a philosophy, and so on, but not a religion.

Yet some people do in fact engage in Buddhism in what appear to be traditional religious ways. They worship the Buddha and hold a variety of supernatural beliefs. Those who hold the No position argue that this is a corruption or misunderstanding of the essence of Buddhism, that is, an inappropriate departure from Buddhism as taught by the Buddha himself and by the most admired practitioners through history. In the often antireligious and secular culture of the contemporary West, this argument is very attractive. It allows Buddhism to avoid criticisms that other religions must face.

Proponents of the Yes position have just as much going for them. Buddhism is a religion if you adopt virtually any definition of religion other than one insisting on the centrality of a creator God. If religion refers to the thoughts, activities, and institutions that bind a group of people together in their existential response to the meaning of life, then Buddhism would be as much a religion as any other. If religion represents the ultimate concerns of people, then Buddhists are religious. The fact that Buddhism emphasizes practice over belief would not make it unusual among the world's religions, nor would the fact that Buddhism is fundamentally a response to human suffering. Buddhism articulates a view or a variety of views on the afterlife. As in other religions, the role of faith (as commitment, confidence, and trust) is central to Buddhist practice. And Buddhist practice is very often connected to images of divine beings whose grace ameliorates suffering and inspires courage, whether these deities are regarded as independently existing beings or as meditative tools to expand the mind.

The fact that Buddhism differs from every religion that preceded it by not being grounded in particular ethnic or cultural bonds, that it was from the outset open to all people regardless of ethnicity, language, and culture, is an intriguing point. Prior to Buddhism, all known religions were based on ethnic identity. Buddhism broke that pattern by making itself available to anyone regardless of tribal identity as a means of enlightening self-transformation—the quest for nirvana. That might have been a good argument not to consider Buddhism a religion had it not been for the fact that religions founded after Buddhism, most notably Christianity and Islam, were similarly disconnected from their earlier ethnocentrism. Taking these points into account, there are solid reasons to consider Buddhism a religion.

Proponents of the third position, that the question is misleading, can also mount a strong case. We saw in the two positions just articulated that a lot depends on the definition of religion that you adopt or presuppose in pondering this question. Whether or not something seems religious to you depends on the breadth of your exposure and on the way the word *religion* has been used by people around you. It also depends on what aspect of Buddhism you're looking at. For almost two and a half millennia, Buddhism has been many things to many people in a wide range of different cultures. That realization helps us see that the question isn't quite as substantial as it may have seemed at first glance, nor as easily answered.

But then, we might still be tempted to ask, "How about people in Asia? Did they think of Buddhism as a religion or not?" Considering this question in terms of the variety of Asian languages and cultures, we realize that for thousands of years Asians never raised this question because they didn't have a word or a concept of religion that matches those in European languages and cultures. Nor, for a long time, did they have a word that corresponds to *Buddhism*. What held their attention was the dharma. Moreover, they were able to think of the dharma as multiple and always expanding "dharma doors," very different ways for different people to seek enlightenment. So if Buddhists were able to avoid the temptation to force everyone into narrow, preordained categories, perhaps we can too. Almost as puzzling as a Zen koan, Buddhism could just be Buddhism.

5.2. Why is Buddhism currently of interest around the world?

Global interest in Buddhism among people whose family and cultural background was not originally Buddhist has tended to focus on two dimensions of the tradition. The first is an open-ended philosophy of life that provides guidance in understanding who we are and how we might go about living wise and ethical lives. Several aspects of this view of the dharma appear to contemporary people to align very well with the challenges of human beings today. Second, among those who have taken an interest in Buddhism are those attracted to practices of meditative mindfulness. Meditation offers concrete possibilities for personal growth and healing, and these meditative exercises can be put into practice by anyone, anywhere. That prospect has drawn many people toward Buddhism.

One frequently given reason for attraction to Buddhism is that Buddhism is the religion that doesn't always seem like a religion. Buddhism interests some people because from a contemporary point of view it seems better equipped to avoid at least some of the most archaic and objectionable dimensions of other religions. Theism is the component of religion most frequently mentioned in this respect. In Buddhism, beliefs about God, gods, divine Buddhas, and so on are neither required nor forbidden. It's entirely optional. From the very beginning to today, there have been many practitioners for whom the existence of divine beings is simply irrelevant. Their practice of Buddhism is aimed at the alleviation of unnecessary suffering or the expansion and transformation of mind, both individual and collective, or on any number of prominent aspects of Buddhism, but not on theistic worship.

Another factor that draws interest to Buddhism is its relation to modern science. Many Buddhists have little difficulty harmonizing the dominant scientific view of the universe with their beliefs and practices. Indeed, Buddhists often claim that there is little or no contradiction between the most important elements of a Buddhist worldview and those of contemporary science. To support this claim they direct attention to the Buddhist teachings of impermanence, dependent arising, the lack of an essential core to all things, and the interdependence of all elements of reality—all of which are now simply assumed in contemporary science. Because of these aspects of a Buddhist worldview the task of coordinating this understanding with evolutionary biology, for example, has been relatively easy for Buddhists. Few Buddhists have felt compelled to mount a harsh criticism of evolution.

The rise of contemporary psychology has also been a boon to Buddhism. Buddhists tend to treat their practice as a kind of therapy. Human problems are understood to arise from delusion; they are issues of misunderstanding, a failure to see things clearly rather than matters of sin or disobedience. For over two millennia Buddhists have been studying and recording all the ways that people's minds have been conditioned by disruptive habits that distort the way they see the world. Mindfulness meditation is regarded as a practical tool to undermine these delusions. Practices such as these are opportunities for anyone to see internal problems, patterns of greed, aversion, and delusion that lead to suffering for oneself and others. These and several other aspects of Buddhism have drawn increased attention to this tradition in the late twentieth and twenty-first centuries.

5.3. How does Buddhism compare to other major world religions in terms of its age and number of participants?

Among the five major world religions—Hinduism, Buddhism, Judaism, Christianity, and Islam—Hinduism has the earliest beginnings, and dating those origins is virtually impossible, but it is at least four thousand years old. Judaism is also difficult to date, but we have good reasons to regard it as the next of these five religions to emerge after Hinduism, whether that dating process focuses on the earliest gathering of the Israelites or on the compilation of the Torah in the sixth century BCE.

Buddhism occupies the middle historical position between these two and the subsequent emergence of Christianity and Islam, dating from sometime in the middle of the fifth century BCE. It is the first world religion to have a distinct founder with a biography that is partially traceable. Several centuries later Christianity emerges through the life of one distinct individual, Jesus of Nazareth, about whom we can know perhaps slightly more than we can about the Buddha, although details are speculative based as they are on later second- and third-hand reports. Islam came into existence six centuries after Christianity, inspired by its prophet, Muhammad, who lived from 570 to 632.

The question of numbers of participants in these religions is much more difficult to answer in a rigorous way. How many Buddhists live in the world today, or Christians or Muslims, depends on who would legitimately qualify to be counted among them. Is being born in a predominantly Buddhist country sufficient to count someone as a Buddhist? Does being a Buddhist require that a person attend temple services on occasion, and how often would that be? To count as a Buddhist is it necessary for someone to be willing to admit that to an official statistician?

The Pew Foundation claims that the world is 7% Buddhist, with Christianity the largest religion, at 31%, and Islam next at 24%. They count less than 20% of Chinese people today as Buddhists but give no indication about how they arrived at this figure. No doubt they consulted the Chinese government census statistics. But the question of the relative size of religions today is sometimes politically motivated and always difficult to judge.

Which religions are still growing in population size today? Probably all of them, given the continued growth in the number of human beings on the planet. What about Buddhism? There are converts all over the world, including in China, now that restrictions on traditional Buddhism have been significantly eased. Does secularization in Buddhist countries like Japan and Korea mean that these numbers are in decline? Yes, in part, but again this is a question of who counts as a Buddhist. If your family heritage is Buddhist but you now live away from home as a business executive and don't participate in any Buddhist activity, are you still a Buddhist? Our answer to this and other questions will affect our statistics substantially.

5.4. How does Buddhism relate to government and politics?

The politics of Buddhism across history and geography cannot be easily summarized. But a few examples may offer a general sense. Although the Buddha organized the Buddhist community, the sangha, to be wholly independent of government, both the Buddha himself and the sangha would inevitably be connected to the state. These connections were always precarious. For the most part an unspoken agreement prevailed: so long as the Buddhist community did not meddle in government affairs (criticize the government, side with groups in opposition to the government, advocate for political reform, etc.), the state would allow its existence, even consider Buddhism a benefit to the society and offer what support it could.

This arrangement has varied from ruler to ruler and from country to country. But a major turning point in the success of early Buddhism was the conversion to Buddhism of Emperor

Ashoka of the Mauryan Empire, which dominated South Asia in the early centuries of Buddhism. Following a particularly brutal conquest, Ashoka began to see himself as the leader who would put Buddhist principles into political effect as the sangha's foremost lay supporter. While he avoided suppression of other religious groups, Ashoka's advocacy and support of Buddhism helped the religion to thrive.

Similar arrangements helped Buddhism to attain prevalence in other cultures. The downside of government support and involvement in religion is well known to us. State influence over and interference in religious decisions—even control over religious leaders—has frequently served to undermine the legitimacy of a religious tradition. Governments can rarely resist the temptation to call upon religious leaders to endorse its actions. When war is declared mutual support between the two is virtually irresistible. In spite of its overtly apolitical stance, Buddhists have fallen prey to all of these dangers on numerous occasions. Buddhist support for Japanese imperialism throughout Asia before and during the Second World War, and Buddhist legitimization of government suppression of Tamil Hindus in Sri Lanka and Rohingya Muslims in Myanmar are just the most recent cases in point.

One new direction in Buddhist interaction with government, now called "engaged Buddhism," is probably among the most important developments in contemporary Buddhism. As Asian governments adopt new and more democratic forms, and as the belief in universal human rights becomes more widespread, Buddhists have become more likely to express political and social views, sometimes regarding them as moral implications of the dharma. When a Vietnamese monk sitting in meditation set himself on fire to protest the suffering and killing in the Vietnam War, other monks joined the protest. One, Thich Nhat Hanh, took the lead in protesting all aspects of the war and the Vietnamese government's involvement. He called upon all Buddhist monks to stage nonviolent protests and to confront the government directly about the suffering caused by its actions.

Buddhist leaders in other Asian nations and increasingly in the West have been inspired by the courageous lead of the Vietnamese monks to risk outspoken positions on a wide variety of social ills. Whenever suffering is being needlessly caused, some Buddhists now feel the obligation to address it directly and to refuse traditional positions of nonconfrontation. Socially engaged Buddhists now promote political involvement in connection to government actions and policies but also in relation to human suffering and planetary degradation caused by corporations. Buddhists' relationship to politics has undergone a recent and perhaps momentous transformation.

5.5. What is the relationship between Buddhism and modern science, and why is this connection so frequently emphasized today?

Assertions that Buddhism is at least compatible with modern science, if not itself a form of scientific inquiry, have circulated for well over a century. When Buddhism first became fashionable in Europe and America in the 1860s, one important aspect of its popularity was a sense that, unlike Western religions, Buddhism was fully in accord with science because it encouraged rather than refused critical, rational thinking based on available evidence. Some admirers went so far as to claim that by condemning dogmatism Buddhism had proved that it was not a religion at all.

These claims of compatibility between Buddhism and science resurfaced with added strength in the second half of the twentieth century. Best-selling books such as *The Tao of Physics* demonstrated in considerable detail how findings in contemporary physics and elsewhere in the sciences had been anticipated by Buddhist (and Daoist) insights, not just by centuries but by millennia. Then, in 1979, a groundbreaking conference at the

Naropa Institute in Colorado organized by cognitive and computer scientists interested in Buddhism initiated what is now a long-standing dialogue between Buddhists and scientists.

Several such conferences have been attended by or hosted by the Dalai Lama, who has taken an interest in modern science throughout his life. At one such meeting he declared that if a Buddhist idea were to be conclusively disproven by scientific investigation, Buddhists would need to reevaluate that idea, no matter how central it had been to traditional Buddhist thinking. The Dalai Lama pointed to the early Buddhist insistence on validation by direct experience and evidence over any counterclaim grounded in scripture or monastic authority. In making this same point, other Buddhists have frequently cited scriptural authority. The Buddha himself is thought to have said, "In the same way that gold should be examined by burning, rubbing, and cutting to verify its true identity, monks and scholars should examine and test my words. Only then should they be believed, rather than simply out of respect for me."

Following early efforts to understand overlapping theories in quantum physics and Buddhist philosophy, a more recent point of emphasis has been the intersection between Buddhist meditation and contemporary neuroscience. Neuroscientists have recently devised experimental methods to measure and evaluate the effects of meditation, including testing the differences in mental effect between advanced meditators and those who are newly engaged in the practice. Numerous articles and books have followed this intriguing intersection, perhaps most notably the best-selling *The Buddha's Brain*.

Not all Buddhists relish these elements of compatibility with science. As with other religions, some Buddhists hold supernatural and theistic beliefs and engage in practices that correspond to them. From their point of view, the Buddhist modernism that seeks to be scientifically relevant surrenders too many aspects of traditional Buddhism that they rely on in their lives.

Some scholars of Buddhism warn that Buddhists should be skeptical about subordinating Buddhist principles to science. When scientific experiments verify traditional Buddhist meditation insight the end result could be that Buddhism is reduced to the role of confirming scientific claims from an alternative point of view. Does Buddhism have something unique to offer the contemporary world? Or will assertions about compatibility end up undermining the possibility that Buddhism may have something of its own to contribute? If Buddhism comes to be considered "a pure science of mind and matter," as one modern Buddhist teacher has claimed, will that have the effect of subordinating it to science? Both the intersection of Buddhism and science and these recent doubts about that intersection are important matters of current debate.

5.6. Isn't there a conflict between basic Buddhist values and the character of modern capitalism?

There are good reasons to think that our initial answer to this question should be "Yes, Buddhist values may very well be at odds with the values of a capitalist economy." Consider this well-known passage from an early Buddhist sutra: "Oh monks, if people know the result of giving and sharing they would not eat without having given, nor would they allow the stain of greed to obsess them and take root in their minds." From the very beginning, Buddhists praised the renunciation of ordinary life, rejected overt materialism, gave forceful critiques of craving, attachment, and greed, and valorized the selfless postures of generosity and compassion. If capitalism is grounded in some form of materialism, if it claims selfishness as the foundation of human nature and assumes that greed is the motivating force of economic advancement, the conflict is obvious.

In spite of this, however, capitalism has been rapidly absorbed into the lives of present and former Buddhist nations. The citizens of India, Thailand, Singapore, China, Korea, and Japan, for example, have had little difficulty taking up capitalist economic thinking and practices. They have done so with notable success and without coming to the conclusion that their underlying Buddhist values must be jettisoned. How might we address this? Is the tension between Buddhism and capitalism irreconcilable, or might it even be a productive tension, one that will prove useful to both sides?

Looking more closely at the ideals of Buddhism we find several paths for the reconciliation of Buddhist values and some form of capitalist economy. Although we assume that renunciation entails rejecting what one wants, a demand to give up something that really does have significant value, at a more mature level Buddhist renunciation evolves out of a comprehensive insight. It entails seeing things as they really are as opposed to seeing things as we might prefer them to be. The Buddhist goal is to renounce not everything but what one can now see to be inessential or even destructive. The point of the Buddhist renunciation of desires is to avoid being controlled by them, to be capable of choosing among desires. Are they conducive to health? Do they accord with the values of wisdom and compassion? The Buddhist goal, then, is not to transcend the world through ascetic renunciation but to see the world as it really is and to live skillfully within it. The truth, they realized, will set you free.

One traditional model for this kind of renunciation within the world is the lay Buddhist businessman Vimalakirti, whose worldly renunciation is described in an early Mahayana sutra. The text claims that Vimalakirti was "engaged in all sorts of businesses yet had no interest in profit or possessions" and that he was "honored as the businessman among businessmen because he demonstrated the priority of the dharma. He was honored as the landlord among landlords because he renounced the aggressiveness of ownership." Creating this model of character for the world of commerce and wealth, Buddhist writers imagined a form of nonattachment that did not require asceticism. It is possible to possess worldly things without being possessed by them.

What these writers sought to articulate was freedom from the enslavement that accumulation and greed can bring about. One of the basic premises of Buddhist practice is that, through meditative exercises, greed could be transformed into generosity, hatred into compassion, and delusion into wisdom, and that this transformation takes place within the world rather than beyond it. Aligned with this belief, greed is regarded as a common human condition but not the bedrock of human nature, since it can be overcome. This is one way that Buddhists have expressed their ideals so that they don't necessarily come into conflict with the structure of capitalism.

At the same time, considerable skepticism about the dangers of capitalist values can be found throughout the history of Buddhist thought and practice. To the extent that capitalism tends to promote the commodification of all aspects of human life and reduce human beings to consumers, Buddhist criticisms have been and will be harsh. The point of life is not consumption, nor is that the path to happiness. In fact, the earliest truths of Buddhism announce clearly that although we inevitably assume otherwise, the fulfillment of desires is not the path to happiness. Happiness is found instead in freedom from enslavement to desires and the freedom to choose among motivations in such a way that healthy living is enhanced. Out-of-control desires give rise to out-of-control suffering. On these grounds there is no getting around the basic Buddhist conviction that greed is the first of three life-threatening poisons. Greed kills. The essential Buddhist condition for happiness is the ability to discipline oneself, to place limits on one's desires so that they enhance life and support the common good.

In a now famous quip, the philosopher Slavoj Žižek muses via Karl Marx that Western Buddhism has now taken on the role of the "opiate of the masses" insofar as its focus on mindful stress reduction keeps hardworking Western capitalists on the job without breakdown or complaint. In this tongue-in-cheek comment, Buddhism turns out to be fully compatible with capitalism even to the point of being essential to its continuation. And so goes the debate. Newly emerging topics such as "Buddhist economics" and "Silicon Valley Buddhism" are now ubiquitous on the internet. Although the economic implications of Buddhism were rarely spelled out in the tradition, these topics are now at the forefront of contemporary Buddhist conversation.

5.7. What is the relationship between Buddhism and modern psychology?

The modern discipline of psychology was born in the nineteenth century at roughly the same time that Buddhism was coming to be known in the West. From that time forward both psychologists and Buddhists have recognized significant common ground. At the beginning of the twentieth century, having listened intently to a Harvard lecture by a Sri Lankan Buddhist, the psychologist and philosopher William James made the offhand prediction that within a quarter-century many people in the West would be studying Buddhist psychology. Although the timing in James's prediction was off by almost a century, Buddhist meditation and philosophy have certainly come to be a factor in the discipline of psychology. To take just one example, Buddhist-style mindfulness practices are now integrated into virtually every form of psychological therapy and are now used to treat stress, anxiety, pain, depression, insomnia, and many other conditions. It is also true that the way contemporary Buddhism has come to be seen in the West borrows heavily on the vocabulary and overall orientation of modern psychology. Buddhists have learned and incorporated a great deal from the discipline of psychology.

Although *Buddhist psychology* is a modern phrase with no traditional counterpart, a focus on and therapeutic treatment of the human psyche goes all the way back to the origins of Buddhism and is heavily emphasized throughout the tradition. Buddhist meditation practice begins with the cultivation of one-pointed concentration, which can then serve as the basis upon which various forms of introspection, mental observation, and therapeutic transformation can proceed. Buddhist meditators learn to observe their own thought processes, emotional states, and patterns of motivation, all of which ordinarily proceeds without conscious recognition. The point of these psychological exercises is to recognize who we are, to tame destructive emotions, and to redirect motivations from the cravings of greed and hatred.

Recall that the early Buddhist understanding of the self is that human beings are highly malleable and open to change. Understanding a person as the ongoing conjunction of five mental and physical components encouraged Buddhists to observe in meditation how each component interacts with the others—how physical perceptions, feelings, thoughts, will, and self-consciousness are always open to influence and change, and how this process can in certain ways be intentionally directed toward enlightened forms of life. This malleability of character allowed Buddhists to observe and study healthy ways of living and to begin to appropriate those into their own lives.

The fact that Buddhist psychology has been embedded in a larger philosophical and religious framework oriented to enlightenment and the cultivation of ethical character has helped make it attractive as a model for the further development of modern Western psychology. Since its beginnings modern psychology has typically been located in the sphere of medicine as the study of psychological illnesses—the range of what can go wrong with human minds. A more persistent focus in Buddhism has been on the positive side of mental life. Its primary questions concern how it might be possible to enhance, expand, and deepen the best states of human character: generosity, openness, creativity, wisdom. Buddhists sought ways to awaken from mental delusions and enslavement to self-imposed suffering in order to focus on the cultivation of greater mental capacity and highly refined states of consciousness.

This alternative psychological model has helped give rise to what is now called "positive psychology," which focuses on the conditions of human flourishing rather than on the diagnosis and treatment of mental illness. Psychologists now emphasize how character traits such as mindfulness and compassion enhance overall well-being and how these traits can be cultivated through the adoption of meditative practice. Buddhism has provided a model for psychologists seeking to address what is possible for human beings and even for envisioning how human evolution might extend beyond what we now take to be "human nature."

While psychologists have used Buddhism and meditation to reenvision their discipline, Buddhists have similarly been able to employ many facets of modern psychology as a means of reengaging with their own earlier traditions. Many Buddhists now recognize how the early Buddhist way of analysis, which focused on understanding inner mental life, had slipped into the background of Buddhist practice and how its resurgence can help make Buddhist ideas relevant to the contemporary cultural world. The recent emergence of what in psychology is called cognitive behavioral therapy, which shares many insights and strategies with Buddhist meditation therapy, has been particularly influential in Buddhist psychology. The discipline of mindfulness-based cognitive therapy shows the extent to which mindfulness meditation from Buddhism has melded with contemporary cognitive therapy.

The language of experience-dependent neuroplasticity is a scientific articulation of what traditional Buddhists had taken as the foundations of meditative practice. That the neurological structure of the brain is plastic, in the sense of malleable, and that it reshapes itself based on habits of experience is precisely what Buddhists had assumed as the basis of its practice.

Buddhists have found the analytical terminology of modern psychology to be very useful in their own practices. Modern psychological terms appear frequently in contemporary Buddhist discussions and help lend both precision and credibility to Buddhist descriptions of meditation. Some Buddhists have begun to recognize how the language and insights of psychology have helped provide them with new ways of looking at their own traditional meditation practices. Psychology and neuroscience are influencing the Buddhist sense of what meditation is and could be.

The use of advanced technology for neuroimaging in hospitals and laboratories is another recent area of importance in Buddhism. EEG brain-wave measurement and functional MRI videos of brain processes are now being used to test and measure the effects of meditation. Neuroimaging for both beginning meditators and advanced practitioners helps researchers understand what it is that meditation can contribute to mental health. Although these tests will likely become more sophisticated over time, results so far show that the benefits of meditation are extensive.

Some Buddhists have expressed reservations about the extent and validity of Buddhism's alignment with modern psychology. They worry that seeing Buddhism through the lens of psychology might have the effect of undermining or obscuring Buddhism's radical liberating effects. They maintain that traditional Buddhism is built on a different set of values and goals and that conflating them will ultimately be detrimental to Buddhism. Some psychologists avoid making any connection to Buddhism on the grounds that connection to a religion could have the effect of throwing the scientific, medical, and secular status of the discipline into question. Nevertheless this connection continues to strengthen today, and the likelihood of greater cooperation is strong.

5.8. What is secular Buddhism, and how has Buddhism adjusted to the overall secular character of contemporary global society?

Secular Buddhism names a newly emerging orientation within Western Buddhism that may become attractive to Asians as well. This version of Buddhism is being articulated by converts seeking to avoid what they see as the perils of Western religions. Although there is no consensus on what secular Buddhism is, participants tend to maintain a scientifically attuned worldview that is nontheistic, naturalistic, humanistic, pragmatic, and agnostic on traditional religious claims about life after death in other worlds. Secular Buddhists focus on meditation and the elements of Buddhist thought that provide instruction on living healthy lives in this world. They de-emphasize or criticize supernatural beliefs, otherworldly concerns, traditional rituals, and the necessity of monastic guidance wherever those appear in the Buddhist tradition.

There are cultural motives for the emergence of secular Buddhism that can be seen in the history of Western Buddhism. In the early decades of Western Buddhist practice, converts would typically join an organization led by a teacher from Asia. Without knowing much about the differences between forms of Buddhism, Westerners began receiving teachings that were either Tibetan, Japanese, Thai, or some other tradition. Converts were often given an Asian Buddhist name and proceeded to learn Buddhism as it had developed in the background culture of that particular teacher. Over time some practitioners found themselves frustrated with several aspects of this way of being a Buddhist.

One frustration had to do with the extent to which Buddhist teachings were inevitably conjoined with a particular Asian culture such that converts felt they were expected to convert not just to Buddhist teachings and practices but to Tibetan or Japanese culture. They wanted to be Buddhist but in a French way or an English way. For some Western Buddhists cultural difference was part of the attraction, while for others this cultural shift seemed neither desirable nor possible.

Another problem for some Western Buddhist converts was that their own grounding in secular, scientific, democratic culture was deeply entrenched and thus nonnegotiable. So whenever Buddhist ideas or practices from Asia appeared to be in tension with that dominant Western cultural orientation it was Buddhism that would need to make the adjustment. Traditional Buddhist beliefs concerning rebirth, other worlds, or supernatural beings to whom one might pray were frequently discarded on grounds of insufficient evidence. Traditional monastic hierarchical structures, assumptions about patriarchy, and other political differences were open grounds for criticism. The available responses to these points of tension were basically three: abandon Buddhism, work for reform within the lineage of an inherited Asian tradition, or found new Buddhist organizations that are at the outset fully Western and contemporary in outlook. Those who have chosen this last option are at the forefront of the creation of secular Buddhism.

Secular Buddhism is clearly part of a larger movement sometimes known as "secular spirituality," a tendency in contemporary Western cultures to seek personal guidance for a spiritually oriented philosophy without the requirement of participation in a traditional religious institution or the adoption of traditional religious beliefs. This naturalized form of spirituality emphasizes personal development, inner peace, and stability in tune with contemporary science and culture, rejecting otherworldly concerns about life after death and the assumption of divine beings overseeing the world. Secular Buddhism shares these concerns, including the insistence that the human search for personal and collective meaning is essential.

Several criticisms of secular Buddhism have appeared:

- That it risks losing the depth of Buddhism as it conforms to science and secularity, becoming diluted or banal.
- That it too quickly cuts off the benefits Westerners might inherit from Asia and hasn't learned enough from earlier Asian forms of Buddhism to begin creating new models.
- That it is based on a misunderstanding of religion by identifying religion with the forms that it has taken in the West, thus shortcutting the potential of contemporary

religion. In recognition of this possibility, Stephen Batchelor, the most prominent advocate of secular Buddhism, has repeatedly claimed that there is an important religious dimension to secular Buddhism.

• That the critique of religious institutions often naively assumes that a spiritual dimension to culture can flourish without institutional support, or that it fails to recognize that whatever new institutions are eventually adopted will very likely be vulnerable over time to the same forms of corruption.

As secular Buddhists address these skeptical responses, the Buddhism they advocate will grow in refinement. Because so many people around the world now encounter Buddhist teachings and practices in secular circumstances—particularly as mindfulness meditation exercises in schools, hospitals, businesses, and even the military—the ease with which they can be utilized outside of religious institutions bodes well for the future of secular Buddhism.

5.9. Who is the Dalai Lama?

Tenzin Gyatso, the fourteenth and current Dalai Lama, is the world's best-known living Buddhist and possibly the most widely recognized human being on the planet. *Dalai Lama* is a title given to the religious leader of Tibetan Buddhism. Although a member of one particular sect of Tibetan Buddhism (the Gelug, or Yellow Hat, lineage), the Dalai Lama represents the unity of all Tibetan sects and the cohesion of the Tibetan people. All those who have held the title of Dalai Lama are considered to be reincarnations of the Mahayana bodhisattva of compassion (Avalokitesvara).

Tenzin Gyatso was born into a humble farming family in rural Tibet. Selected by Tibetan Buddhist leaders at a very young age and given the highest form of Buddhist education, the Dalai Lama was pressed into office while still a teenager because of increasing Chinese political and military threats to Tibetan autonomy. In 1959 the Dalai Lama escaped from Tibet along with other Buddhist leaders to take up residence in Dharamsala in northwestern India.

As the symbolic leader of Tibet, the Dalai Lama has faced enormous political pressure. For many years he sought the liberation of Tibet from Chinese dominance. As that goal became increasingly unlikely, by the 1980s the Dalai Lama conceded overall sovereignty to China while seeking enough autonomy for Tibetan culture to thrive on its own terms. At the time of this writing it has been sixty years since the Dalai Lama last set foot in Tibet.

Exiled from Tibet and the position of direct leadership there, the Dalai Lama has traveled the world as the foremost representative of Tibet and, in some sense, of Buddhism. He has authored many books, has given public talks all over the world, and has become an influential teacher of meditation and Buddhist philosophy. He is known for his lifelong interest in science, his sense of humor, and his ability to make almost immediate connections with a wide range of people; no public speaker has attracted the enormous audiences that the Dalai Lama has over the past half-century. The story of his life was depicted in a major motion picture in 1997 under the direction of Martin Scorsese, and his books have sold many millions of copies. For most non-Buddhists, the Dalai Lama is the face of Buddhism.

As he enters the final segment of his life, much controversy surrounds the future of the institution of the Dalai Lama. Long opposed to positions taken by the fourteenth Dalai Lama and irritated by his global prominence, the Chinese government insists on some degree of control over who will be chosen as the next Dalai Lama, an insistence resisted by Tibetan Buddhist leaders both inside and outside Tibet. The Dalai Lama himself has equivocated, claiming on occasion that he just might be the last in the lineage and that the institution of the Dalai Lama might have outlived its usefulness. On another occasion the

Dalai Lama said that his rebirth would not take place in any territory controlled by the Chinese government, and on yet another occasion it was suggested that in case of a controversy on this matter the Tibetan people might have to decide the issue by democratic vote.

Meanwhile, toward the end of his life it is clear that the fourteenth Dalai Lama has become an international figure of great importance, indeed among the most highly respected and beloved people in the world. He has become a symbol of peaceful, nonviolent negotiation between peoples and, although officially representing only a tiny fraction of Buddhists, is now widely accepted as a leading figure of the Buddhist tradition even by Buddhists of other nationalities. This kind of cross-cultural status is unique in the history of Buddhism.

5.10. Who are the other most widely known or important Buddhist leaders?

There are many significant Buddhist leaders of the twentieth and twenty-first centuries. Here are four who have been especially prominent in very different ways and styles:

Thich Nhat Hanh is a Vietnamese Buddhist monk, meditation teacher, and peace activist who has attracted millions of followers all over the world. His teachings are drawn from many segments of the Buddhist tradition: early Pali sutras, Mahayana philosophy, Zen, and even Western psychology and environmentalism. Nhat Hanh first came to international attention for his opposition to the Vietnam War. Coining the now well-known term *engaged Buddhism*, he has made the case that committed Buddhists should be active participants in the political debates of their time. In 1966, while in the US to attend a symposium and to visit Thomas Merton and Martin Luther King Jr., Nhat Hanh was informed that he would not be allowed to return to Vietnam. Denied access to his own country, he moved to France to engage in peace activism. In 1967 Martin Luther King Jr. nominated him for the Nobel Peace Prize. In 1982 Nhat Hanh founded the Plum Village Community of Engaged Buddhists in southwest France. It would become his long-term home and the center for his many activities and institutions. Thich Nhat Hanh's monastic order is the Order of Interbeing, in reference to the central Buddhist idea of the interdependence of all elements of reality. Members of the order manage meditation and retreat centers in Europe, the US, and Vietnam. Although Nhat Hanh continued to be denied access to Vietnam after the war, in 2007 he finally returned to his native country to visit monasteries and temples and to teach. He is the author of dozens of widely read books on Buddhism, mindfulness meditation, and numerous other topics, which are published by his own publication house, Parallax Press. In 2014 Nhat Hanh was hospitalized with a brain hemorrhage and has been unable to speak since then. In 2018 he returned to Vietnam to live out the remainder of his life.

S. N. Goenka (1924–2013) was a highly influential Burmese meditation teacher in the Vipassana tradition. After spending much of his career as a businessman in Myanmar, in 1969 he moved to India, from where his reputation for Buddhist teachings spread worldwide. A Buddhist modernist, Goenka emphasized the rational, scientific, and nonsectarian, universal character of the Buddhist path. He encouraged the rejection of traditional ritual and advocated against the imposition of any required beliefs for Buddhists. During his lengthy career, Goenka opened Vipassana meditation centers all over the world, leading meditation retreats that influenced thousands of Buddhists from both Asian and Western backgrounds. Among his many notable Western students are Jack Kornfield, Joseph Goldstein, Sharon Salzberg, and Daniel Goleman, all of whom have been instrumental in the widespread dissemination of Buddhist meditation techniques. Goenka founded the Vipassana Research Institute, which pursued the careful study of Vipassana and became the home base for the translation of early Buddhist sutras from the Pali. Goenka was also influential in introducing meditation practices into prisons and setting up networks of instruction for mental training specifically tailored to the difficulties of prison life.

Shunryu Suzuki (1904–1971) was a monk and teacher in the Soto Zen tradition whose influence on the global growth of Zen practice was extraordinary. Born into the Soto Zen tradition, Suzuki began training in Japan at the age of twelve. He graduated from Komazawa University, the Soto Zen headquarters near Tokyo, and underwent rigorous training at the two primary Soto Zen monasteries, Eihei-ji and Soji-ji. In 1959, at the age of fifty-five, Suzuki was sent to San Francisco to serve immigrant Japanese there as a priest at the Soto Zen temple. At just that historical juncture, Zen was in vogue among the San Francisco beat poets and artists, and soon non-Japanese Americans were studying meditation with Suzuki. Within a few years he would leave his temple assignment to found the San Francisco Zen Center, and from that point on he became the best known Zen master outside of Japan. He founded the first Zen monastery outside of East Asia, in the mountains of California. Under Suzuki's inspirational leadership, the San Francisco Zen Center attracted practitioners from all over the world. *Zen Mind, Beginner's Mind*, a collection of Suzuki's dharma talks, has been a best-selling book for almost half a century and has been a major factor in the expansion of Zen globally.

Chogyam Trungpa (1939–1987) was an acclaimed reincarnated Tibetan lama who, after immigrating to the West and abandoning his monastic status, displayed an uncanny ability to communicate the Buddhist dharma to Western audiences. His book, *Born in Tibet*, recounts his nine-month trek over the Himalayas to India in 1959. This would be the first of many books that would introduce Tibetan Buddhism and Tantra to contemporary European and American youths eager to encounter a version of Buddhism that was tailored specifically to their enthusiasms and their weaknesses. After moving to England to accept a scholarship to Oxford University, Trungpa immigrated to the US in 1970. He is credited with founding over one hundred Shambhala Meditation Centers and the first Buddhist University in North America, Naropa University in Boulder, Colorado. At Naropa, Trungpa brought a long list of important artists, poets, and philosophers, including Allen Ginsberg and William Burroughs, to teach alongside him. The list of Trungpa's famous students encompasses musicians David Bowie and Joni Mitchell as well as the poet Anne Waldman. Chogyam Trungpa's unconventional and challenging teaching style led to frequent controversy. By the 1980s his health was rapidly failing as a result of an earlier car accident and his heavy consumption of alcohol. He died in his late forties, in 1987.

5.11. What positions have Buddhist leaders taken on issues of violence, war, and peace?

Buddhist teachings are very clear about the necessity of avoiding all forms of violence. The central virtue of noninjury is frequently discussed in the early sutras, and the very first precept for Buddhists is "Avoid killing or harming any living being." The Three Poisons name greed and hatred as the causes of violence, and the third poison, delusion, directs Buddhists away from the false assumption that peace can be attained through violence. The sutras have the Buddha say "If you turn your mind to hostility you do not follow my teaching" and "Hatred will not cease by hatred, but by love alone. This is the ancient law." Thus it is reported that when Emperor Ashoka converted to Buddhism he repented of his violent military conquests and vowed a reign of peace. Even when the martial arts are practiced by Buddhists, as they were in the famous Shaolin temple in China, the monk's code of limitation on violence or outright avoidance was clear. Among all the world's religions, Buddhism has a well-deserved reputation for nonviolence.

In spite of the clarity of these teachings, however, violence may have been as frequent and as bloody in the history of Buddhist nations as in others. Just focusing on recent history, we see Japanese Buddhist leadership affirming and supporting military aggression throughout Asia both before and during World War II, Buddhist monks involved in various forms of political violence in Thailand, and an aggressive Buddhist-backed military campaign to suppress the Tamil Hindu presence in Sri Lanka throughout its protracted civil war.

More recently Myanmar has provided a stark example of Buddhist failure to enact the tradition's own principles of nonviolence and compassion. In the summer of 2017, when Rohingya Muslim militants attacked police checkpoints in Rakhine province, the army of this Buddhist-majority nation retaliated with immediate and excessive violence, killing and injuring thousands of Muslim residents along with some Rohingya Hindus, burying them in mass graves, and driving others from their homes. Huge numbers of Rohingya Muslims crossed the border into Bangladesh, where, at the time of this writing, there are still over a million living in squalid refugee camps.

Although the United Nations negotiated with Myanmar to allow Rohingya Muslims to return, no guarantee was given that they could return to their homes or to their villages, some of which had been completely destroyed. Although this treatment of minority populations is not officially Buddhist, some Buddhist leaders and monks in Myanmar have given the military their full support. There is a rising tide of Burmese Buddhist nationalism that seeks to "reestablish" the country as a Buddhist nation. While Buddhist leaders elsewhere, including the Dalai Lama and Thich Nhat Hanh, have condemned this violence against Muslims, within Myanmar Buddhist resistance to the military regime has been largely impotent. It is clear that Buddhism's reputation for compassion and nonviolence has been tarnished.

It is natural to ask how Buddhists, whose tradition is so thoroughly oriented to the avoidance of aggression and violence, could have so frequently failed to live in accordance with their professed beliefs. Buddhists turn to their own teachings for a variety of answers to that question. The most important of these is that everyone, Buddhist and non-Buddhist alike, is vulnerable to the Three Poisons of greed, hatred, and delusion. Although we may pride ourselves on our compassionate beliefs about the welfare of others, living fully in accord with those ideals, especially in a time of crisis or when our own interests must be sacrificed, is another matter. From a Buddhist point of view, our beliefs will almost inevitably collapse under pressure if we have not undertaken the disciplinary exercises necessary to internalize those ideals. This essential step requires the cultivation of character, and while in Buddhism that is the function of meditative practice, it is clear that for a variety of reasons most Buddhists have not managed that achievement.

Buddhists do have exemplars to follow and to provide instruction in these disciplines, the Dalai Lama and Thich Nhat Hanh foremost among them. And now there is also an international organization specifically formed to address issues of peace and nonviolence from a Buddhist point of view. The Buddhist Peace Fellowship, founded in 1978, takes the following as its mission statement: "Aware of the interconnectedness of all things, the Buddhist Peace Fellowship cultivates the conditions for peace, social justice, and environmental sustainability within ourselves, our communities, and the world."

5.12. What can we learn from Buddhism about nature and the environment? What are ecoBuddhism and Green Buddhism?

Although traditional Buddhists were certainly not environmentalists in our contemporary sense, central elements in the Buddhist worldview lend themselves to environmentalism. Fundamental to this perspective is a Buddhist understanding of the thoroughgoing interdependence of all elements of reality. While all beings are impermanent and in motion, everything connects in some way to everything else. This perspective puts more emphasis on the relationships between things than on the individual things themselves. Buddhists understand human beings to be integrated into the natural world rather than segregated from it, and we are as subject to impermanence, dependent arising, and ultimate selflessness as any other creatures.

This environmentally friendly view of the world is probably most highly developed in East Asian Buddhism. We can get a glimpse of this way of seeing the world in a traditional Buddhist/Daoist-inspired landscape scroll painting. Mountaintops emerge out of mists, streams with cascading waterfalls link different elevations, forests of different species blend into one another, and a few human beings and small villages can be spotted nestled into the whole. Viewers find their gaze moving from one section of the landscape to another, through a bamboo grove into a meadow and up into pines that are all linked together as one vast ecosystem. This big-picture, relational perspective helps support ethical restraint insofar as each of us can see ourselves as intimately connected to others and supported by all things. Although most Buddhists are probably not vegetarians, the ideal of a vegetarian diet is based on the moral standard of noninjury to all sentient beings and a sense of respect for our shared world.

The development of these aspects of Buddhist thought into a globally responsible environmental ethics for our time is one of the most noticeable dimensions of contemporary Buddhism. While committed to retaining a solid grounding in the Buddhist practices of mindful awareness and simplicity of lifestyle, activists in what is now called ecoBuddhism or Green Buddhism have been at the forefront of discussions about the environmental crisis that now confronts all of us. Although there is certainly no unanimity of approach, Buddhists engaged in these issues begin with a critique of the consumer culture that has spread from the US across the world.

These Buddhists have recognized that all cultures—not just Asian cultures—traditionally praised frugality and simplicity of life. But with the rise of modern economics, grounded as it is in productivity, desire-based consumerism, and the goal of perpetual expansion, these traditional values were thoroughly undermined. Buddhists have criticized the role of debt and the anxiety that comes with it, along with the waste that is generated by the desire for bigger, better, and newer everything. They claim that advertising intentionally promotes dissatisfaction throughout life while offering an illusory cure that amounts to self-absorption in the latest styles.

From a Buddhist point of view, this is an unhealthy value system. It misleads us by distorting our actual situation in the world. Buddhist critics claim that consumer culture is toxic for the environment and that the integrity of life itself is threatened by our self-destructive practices. Their point is that consumerism is a form of delusion because it offers commodities as a solution to what is actually a spiritual problem of meaning and satisfaction in life when the things that we consume cannot possibly fulfill that role.

Although traditional Buddhist language calls for renunciation as an authentic solution to the problem, that negative view of giving up can also be seen from the other side as freedom. Renouncing the addictions of consumption may make it possible to liberate oneself from bondage and confinement. From a Buddhist point of view this occurs through the development of a relationship to things of the world that is free of clinging, a state of mind not consumed by the flames of impulse and greed. It comes into being through the disciplines of awareness, contentment, and equanimity. To set oneself free from craving, seeking, and clinging opens a space in life for gratitude, appreciation, and composure.

In this sense, Buddhist eco-activism is characteristically grounded in inner work; changing the outer world of our environment is possible only by transforming the inner world from heedlessness to mindfulness. Activists have made clear that creating an adequate Buddhist response to our environmental crisis entails the creation of a new way of life for human beings. Leading spokespeople like Thich Nhat Hanh and Joanna Macy warn environmental activists that neither fear nor anger will do as a response to the severity of this problem, and that activists will succeed only to the extent that they act out of deep understanding and compassion. Gary Snyder, whose essays and poetry have defined the leading edge of Buddhist eco-activism, has composed a Buddhist sutra to address the crisis. In his tongue-in-cheek "Smokey the Bear Sutra," Snyder imagines the Buddha incarnating as Smokey the Bear, in his blue overalls and brown ranger hat, teaching us wayward consumers of the world how to live lightly on the earth as authentically awakened beings!

5.13. After having virtually disappeared from its country of origin, has Buddhism been revived in modern India?

Buddhism has been gaining momentum in India since the middle of the twentieth century. There are three primary dimensions to this movement: the rapidly growing numbers of tourists from all over Asia in search of the geographical roots of Buddhism, the immigration of large numbers of Tibetan Buddhists to northern India, and the conversions of millions of lower caste Hindu "untouchables" to Buddhism that began in 1956.

The last of these developments accounts for the greatest number of Buddhists in India today. This conversion is credited to the influence of a single individual, Dr. B. R. Ambedkar, who had worked with Gandhi and Nehru to bring about the independence of India and who was also one of the principal architects of the Indian Constitution. Ambedkar was himself a Dalit, a member of the "untouchable" caste, who somehow managed to achieve a college education and eventually law and doctoral degrees. Empowered by his own experience of severe discrimination in the Indian caste system, Ambedkar began to study Buddhism as a means of rejecting its entire structure. He saw the Buddha as a radical reformer who renounced the caste system and taught people how to achieve an egalitarian society. In 1956 Ambedkar publicly converted from Hinduism to Buddhism along with well over a quarter-million other Dalits.

This neo-Buddhist movement continues to grow today, imbued with both religious and political significance. Mass Buddhist conversions of this kind have become important political statements in India, giving a social class lacking in clout a strong sense of political empowerment. The current Hindu nationalist government of India, led by Prime Minister Narendra Modi, has attempted to undermine or to incorporate the Dalit movement. Modi has frequently praised Buddhism, in part to develop common ground with the Buddhist nations that surround India, and when visiting these countries he makes a point of visiting important Buddhist sites.

A second factor in the revival of Buddhism in India is the influx of refugees from Tibet. When the fourteenth Dalai Lama escaped Chinese-controlled Tibet in 1959, tens of thousands of Tibetan Buddhists followed. Large numbers of escaping Tibetans settled in Dharamsala in northern India, where the Dalai Lama eventually made his permanent headquarters, but migrants settled all along the southern edges of the Himalayas, from Ladakh to Darjeeling. Buddhist monasteries and temples in these regions have grown rapidly, and international tourism has increased exponentially as global interest in Tibetan Buddhism has grown. As the political hope for a return to Tibet fades among exiled Tibetans, the image of these northern Indian mountainous areas as distinctly Buddhist grows.

A third development in the revival of Buddhism in India is the rapid rise of interest in the northern Indian plains as the Buddha's original home. This development was spurred by a prominent Sri Lankan Buddhist, Anagarika Dharmapala, who founded the Maha Bodhi Society in the early twentieth century to restore the most significant Buddhist holy places. Bodh Gaya, the location of the Buddha's enlightenment experience, has grown rapidly as a pilgrimage site for millions of Buddhist tourists from all over Asia and now from around the world. This once tiny village now houses dozens of Buddhist temples and monasteries, with monks and nuns from many nations now in permanent residence. Important Buddhist archaeological sites are spread across northern India, and many of these are becoming spiritual tourist attractions. Aware of the economic boon from global tourism, national and local governments in India have helped fund and encourage the restoration of these sites as the holy land for hundreds of millions of Buddhists all over the world.

The most recent census in India put the number of Buddhists at 8.4 million. Buddhist leaders scoff at this figure, claiming both politically motivated and unintentional understatement by tens of millions. Regardless, it is clear that the number of Buddhists in India is growing but also that this group remains a very small minority in a nation that far exceeds a billion people.

5.14. How have Buddhists responded to the easing of restrictions on religion in China?

When Mao Zedong's Communist Revolution founded the People's Republic of China in 1949, Buddhism and religion in general entered a period of forceful suppression. Mao agreed with Marx's position that "religion is the opiate of the people" and that religious professionals were "parasites" living off the sacrifices of workers. But Mao was in too big a hurry to simply allow religion to "wither away," as Marx had advised. Although article 36 of the Chinese Constitution gave citizens "freedom of religious belief" in principle, under Mao freedom of religious practice and expression was entirely forbidden.

In the early 1950s Buddhist properties were confiscated by the government and monastics forced to return to the status of ordinary citizens. Most temples and monasteries were put to new use as hospitals, restaurants, or military barracks. A few of the most famous temples were preserved along with their priceless works of art, but a government-led Chinese Buddhist Association kept very strict control of their activities. Buddhism and other religions, primarily Daoism and Christianity, were essentially shut down.

The situation went from very bad to much worse. During the infamous Cultural Revolution (1966–1976) youthful Red Guards destroyed most of the Buddhist heritage in China on the assertion that it constituted reactionary opposition to socialist progress. Temples and monasteries were reduced to ruins, and Buddhist sculptures, paintings, and ancient sacred texts were burned. The infrastructure supporting Chinese Buddhism was almost entirely gone. For over a quarter of a century no child was raised as a Buddhist in China. After Mao's death in 1976, the government began to reverse its policies on religion, but especially on Buddhism. Chinese citizens were understandably very cautious about any open expression of adherence to Buddhism, since for decades anyone caught practicing or advocating Buddhism was imprisoned or sent to rehabilitation work camps. But as the decades have rolled by without overt government suppression, more and more people have turned to Buddhism, though many of these—anyone under forty—are too young to have had any experience of it in their earlier lives.

The best current statistics on religious affiliation in China come from the Pew Research Center, which estimates that there are 245 million Buddhists in China, or 18% of the total population. Another 21% identify with Chinese folk religious practices that are equal parts Buddhist and Daoist. And this measure counts only those who are willing to risk self-identification, knowing that the government could reverse policy again, putting them in jeopardy. No matter how many get counted as Buddhist, China is now and has long been the most populous Buddhist country in the world.

Current government policy is mostly welcoming toward Buddhism even though the governing Buddhist Association of China keeps a sharp eye on all temple activities. But many Buddhist temples have found it difficult or even impossible to get official government licenses to operate. Although they have been allowed to remain open, they pursue Buddhist practice without official support, knowing that the government can shut them down at any time if they are suspected of antigovernment activity. Temples that have official registrations thrive under government support. The Buddhist Association serves as the official regulatory agency. Their stated assignment is to encourage forms of Buddhist thought and practice that are "intellectually respectable" and not "superstitious." On this policy the Association has sought to ban or discourage incense burning and other devotional offerings as superstitious and not suitable for contemporary religion.

Temples face several problems. One is that government appointees to temple leadership positions are often people who are neither Buddhist nor religious. They are there to ensure obedience to government policy, which creates conditions for Buddhist practice that strike some practitioners as artificial. A second problem is financial. Having lost the wealth that sustained them, temples feel compelled to make money, and some leaders have been stressing wealth creation over spiritual concerns. This has also led to several cases of corruption in which non-Buddhist leaders at temples take advantage of their positions to seek financial gain for themselves.

Beginning in 2006 China has three times hosted a World Buddhist Forum, in which the Chinese delegation has emphasized the "contribution of Buddhism to economic growth and social harmony." These forums and also the new Silk Road development initiative have sought to build relations with China's neighbors through their shared Buddhist heritage.

A great deal of money from outside of mainland China has sponsored the rebuilding of important Buddhist temples.

Contributions have come especially from the Fo Guang Shan Buddhist organization in Taiwan, but also from Japan, Singapore, and the Chinese diaspora communities all over the world. The prospects of a massive influx of Buddhist tourism in the future are great, and although the Chinese government finds itself in a position to bargain for control in order to allow these funds to be collected, the long-term financial benefits are obvious.

While Chinese Buddhism has flourished since Mao, the tradition has yet to produce a Buddhist leader who is revered by the international Buddhist community, someone whose wisdom and compassion are widely admired. It is likely that the coming to maturity of modern Chinese Buddhism will depend upon the quality of leadership that emerges.

5.15. How have Buddhist humanitarian organizations and women's leadership in them begun to transform East Asian Buddhism?

Although Buddhists have cultivated generosity and sympathy for the poor, the sick, and the disabled from the very beginning of the tradition, charitable organizations had not existed within Buddhism until the twentieth century. Perhaps the two most successful Buddhist humanitarian organizations were founded in Taiwan.

The first of these is the Tzu Chu Compassion Relief Association and Foundation, created by an inspired Buddhist nun, the Venerable Cheng Yen. Early in her life Cheng Yen took the bodhisattva vow to pursue awakened well-being on behalf of all living beings. To carry that ultimate mission into action she made a commitment to live simply and to dedicate her life to helping others.

From its modest beginnings in 1966, Cheng Yen's Foundation has grown steadily into one of the world's most successful charitable organizations. Its mission includes providing food, clothing, and medical care to the poor. Numerous hospitals and free clinics have been opened in Taiwan and elsewhere around the world. The Foundation does international relief work and is involved in environmental work and education. Much of the work is performed by Buddhist volunteers who receive training in how to conduct their charitable labor as an explicit form of mindful awareness and compassion. The benefit of their work is understood to be mutual: it gives the recipients an opportunity to attain self-reliance, and it gives the workers an opportunity to deepen their practice of selflessness and love. One of the stated goals of Cheng Yen's modern, updated Mahayana Buddhism is to make active, selfless social work the defining sign of authentic bodhisattva practice.

A second Taiwan-based charitable organization is operated by the Fo Guang Shan Buddhist Order, founded by the Venerable Hsing Yun. What the organization calls "humanistic Buddhism" strives to weave active social engagement into the center of Buddhist religious practice in a manner similar to that practiced by Cheng Yen. The conjoining of self-cultivation and social service in humanistic Buddhism has generated passionate engagement among Chinese Buddhists—especially among women, both nuns and the laity.

Although based in central Taiwan, this organization now has operations in China, the US, and elsewhere. They have opened Buddhist libraries, colleges, and universities. They offer free medical clinics in both urban and remote locations. The organization provides food and clothing for the poor and operates orphanages as well as assisted living homes for the elderly.

These humanitarian organizations and others that have been inspired by their example are a new development in Buddhism. They are remarkable in the extent to which they move Mahayana bodhisattva practice toward a new level of dedication to the concrete demands of their own vows of compassion. Part of the success of these organizations is the way they have been able to offer practitioners a variety of officially sanctioned channels to engage in active bodhisattva practice.

As wealth grows in East Asia it seems likely that this type of Buddhist practice will become more popular.

5.16. What is the status of Buddhism in Tibet? What about Tibetan Buddhism in exile?

It has now been well over a half-century since the Dalai Lama's departure from Tibet. During that lengthy stretch of time he has neither visited his homeland nor been allowed any form of official communication with the people there. Buddhist leadership within Tibet has changed dramatically. Many Tibetan monks have followed their leader in fleeing the country. Others have been killed in conflicts with Chinese military forces, and still others have left Buddhist monastic life either voluntarily or through coercion. Most Buddhist monasteries in Tibet have been destroyed, and although there are still Tibetan monks and nuns, their numbers are kept to easily controllable proportions.

Several Buddhist monasteries and other religious sites are open, but access to them is restricted and carefully controlled by the government. For many years it has been illegal to display images of the Dalai Lama, who has been officially condemned as a "dangerous separatist." Monks and nuns in Tibet have joined in and led protests, but the results have often been imprisonment, sometimes torture. A few monks have resorted to self-immolation in dramatic displays of protest.

Tibetan monks and nuns have been forced to enroll in "patriotic reeducation programs" that reflect the narrative about Tibet favored by the Chinese government. Monastics are expected to admit on public record that Tibet is a part of China and to denounce the Dalai Lama for spearheading the separatist movement. Those who have refused to submit have been ejected from monasteries. For ordinary Tibetan citizens, there are both penalties for refusal to submit and rewards for following the Chinese line. Among the rewards are financial incentives that make failure to accommodate very difficult for Tibetan families.

On its side, Beijing regularly issues denials that it has been guilty of religious intolerance and cultural oppression. The government argues that the occupation of Tibet had liberated the people from enslavement to monastic persecution and the continued imposition of medieval customs. The Chinese occupying forces believe they have made possible Tibet's entrance into the modern world.

To back its claims, China has made a massive investment in Tibet. Infrastructure projects on a scale that Tibetans couldn't possibly have imagined have been under construction throughout the Chinese "economic miracle" of the past quarter-century. Airports, rail lines, and highways have been completed, with more in various stages of design and planning. The new Belt and Road Initiative, by means of which China hopes to reach all the way across Central Asia to Europe, has enhanced the value of Tibet's strategic location at the very center of this region.

A relatively new dimension of China's plans for Tibet includes protecting the historic Buddhist temples and monasteries that remain and rebuilding some of those that were completely destroyed. Hundreds of millions of dollars have been directed toward this undertaking. Reasons for this policy change include the realization that future economic benefits from Tibetan and Buddhist tourism will be substantial, and that this move might help to repair Beijing's damaged reputation for religious oppression, putting it more in line with the government's stated policy of religious pluralism.

With this in mind, major renovations have taken place at the famous Potala Palace, the former residence of the Dalai Lama; at the seventh-century Jokhang temple; and at two of the most important traditional monastic training sites, the Drepung and Sera monasteries. Tourism has already reached 25 million visitors per year—providing a substantial share of Tibetan GNP—and although the majority of these visitors are Chinese, the prospects for international tourism are clearly foremost in the minds of government planners. As Chinese investments and subsidies to the economy have grown, so has the overall wealth

of Tibet. This growth has led some Tibetans to prefer moder-
nity to the traditional culture, which they associate with relative poverty. To whatever extent that preference seems to have
taken hold, the Chinese strategy has accomplished its aims.

Meanwhile, interest in Tibetan Buddhism outside of Tibet
continues to grow, especially in Europe and the US but virtually
everywhere else as well. In spite of denunciation by China, the
Dalai Lama continues to be held in the highest esteem by millions
of people all over the world. Now, ironically, there is growing interest among the Chinese youth in Tibetan-style Buddhism, perhaps in part as a small act of rebellion. In addition, a number of
wealthy Chinese entrepreneurs have openly embraced Tibetan
Buddhism, a sign to other Chinese citizens that this trend is unlikely to be met with strong government opposition.

The material success that many Chinese people have
achieved over the past quarter-century has led to a religious
revival, with growing interest in spiritual traditions that had
no cachet at all through the first half-century of the People's
Republic. So far at least, Tibetan Buddhism is the leading attraction. Tibetan monks, always in need of financial support,
have now begun to travel to China to lead Buddhist services
or to give talks. Some have taken up residence there. Even
more recently, rumors have surfaced that President Xi Jinping
and his wife have taken an interest in Tibetan Buddhism and
that possible changes in official policy may follow. It should be
clear from this summary that the status of Tibetan Buddhism
is highly uncertain and always in process of change, but that
Tibetan Buddhism clearly has something important to offer
that will be in widespread demand.

5.17. How does Buddhism deal with controversial issues like divorce, abortion, and suicide?

Although there are no universal regulations to be found in
Buddhist sutras on these difficult social questions, occasionally some direction for thinking can be gleaned from early and

important texts. This gives each Buddhist culture some leeway in deciding how its own policies might be shaped to align with the overall intent of the dharma. It also allows pre-Buddhist cultures and other traditions of religious and philosophical thought to have some influence on how these matters are decided. Therefore, what we have are somewhat different sets of rules and sensibilities on these issues from one Buddhist country to another.

First, on the question of divorce, because Buddhism was initially a monastic religion that required celibacy of all participants, the Buddha's early sutra talks have very little to say about marriage or divorce. Marriage was a civic matter beyond the purview of Buddhist rules, and although monks and nuns might attend a wedding to sanctify it, they did not conduct marriage ceremonies. Since marriage was not regarded as a sacrament by Buddhists, there are no universal prohibitions on divorce. Among the first five precepts that were thought to be binding on both monastic and lay Buddhists is an admonition against sexual misconduct. For monks and nuns, of course, that means lives without any kind of sexual relations, heterosexual or homosexual. But for the laity it meant loyalty to one's partner in marriage and no extramarital relations, among other things. Buddhist cultures differ to some extent on whether sexual misconduct by one partner in a marriage constitutes grounds for divorce, but under certain circumstances it does. The focus of decision-making on these matters has a lot to do with the Buddhist interest in alleviating suffering. When the termination of a marriage can fulfill that function, all things considered, Buddhists often comply.

Although Buddhist cultures differ on the question of abortion, it is widely agreed that abortion comes with serious karmic consequences. The overarching prohibition on killing any sentient form of life is thought to apply to an unborn fetus, especially in late stages. Monks and nuns were forbidden to assist in abortions, but in many modern Buddhist cultures that prohibition, while still binding, can be overruled by the possible threat to the mother's life. It is recognized that the sanctity of life entails complications of many kinds and the subsequent necessity of compromise even when basic principles are at stake.

Among Buddhists, Tibetans tend to regard abortion as morally unacceptable regardless of circumstances, a position affected by their more rigorous and literal understanding of rebirth. But the global diaspora of Tibetan people has sometimes rendered this more traditional judgment unworkable, and the Dalai Lama's somewhat flexible position, in which the totality of circumstances must be considered, shows this pragmatic turn. It is known that the abortion rate in Myanmar is relatively high. But that statistic seems to reflect the poverty and difficulty of circumstances in Myanmar more than the moral thinking of the citizens, as Buddhist policy there is very firm in denying women access to abortions.

In East Asia—China, Korea, and Japan—abortion is more widely tolerated than in other Buddhist countries. But in official policy that access is limited to cases of rape and risk to a woman's health, even though abortions occur in a much wider range of circumstances than those. When abortions do occur among East Asian Buddhists, there are Buddhist rituals available to deal with the inevitable sense of guilt and the fear of karmic consequences.

Suicide is an issue that the early Buddhist code of monastic life deals with directly. The first and most important precept is to refrain from killing sentient life, including oneself. For a monk or nun to speak to others in praise of death or stressing life's suffering in ways that encourage suicide, or to encourage self-harm in any way, is strictly forbidden. These warnings show that suicide was an issue of some concern in early India and that the Buddhist position on the sanctity of life was the most relevant teaching.

Nevertheless, there are sutra stories that avoid thoroughgoing condemnation of suicide. Some of these focus on cases in which overwhelming suffering appears to be unavoidable.

Because intention plays a major role in discussions of karma, reasons for the contemplation of suicide are given strong consideration in making judgments about suicide victims, especially those suffering from unsustainable physical or emotional pain. In one sutra the Buddha offers some praise for a monk who was so completely overcome with pain that no opportunity for advancement toward nirvana was possible. Another example even goes so far as to suggest that a monk may have attained enlightenment after having committed suicide rather than having been karmically harmed. These cases are clearly exceptional, however. Suicide is firmly prohibited throughout Buddhist traditions even though cultural differences play a major role in determining the kind and degree of reactions.

5.18. What holidays and festivals are celebrated by modern Buddhists, and are there modern pilgrimages that Buddhists consider important?

There are many Buddhist holidays that are occasions for joyous festival celebration or thoughtful contemplation. Almost all of these are local and specific to a particular type of Buddhism or, more often, to one or another ethnic culture within Buddhism. Most Buddhist holidays and festivals are timed to the traditional lunar calendar and therefore occur at different times each year.

The one holiday festival that is shared by all Buddhists is Vesak, often called Buddha's Day, which celebrates the Buddha's birthday and in some traditions his enlightenment and death as well. This holiday occurs on the first full moon in May, with the exception of leap year, when it falls in June. (There is some variation in dates among Japanese Buddhists.) All Buddhist temples take this occasion to stage major celebrations. Lay people flock to temples in large numbers, sometimes staying for the entire day's activities, sometimes just passing through on a brief family outing. Festival foods are served, while some temples take the occasion to distribute free food to the poor. Chanting and dharma talks often take place, but the mood in most cultures tends to be one of joyous celebration.

New Year's celebrations are also common at Buddhist temples, although each culture has its own way of timing that occasion and of celebrating it. In the Theravada countries of Southeast Asia—Thailand, Myanmar, Cambodia, and Laos, but also in Sri Lanka—New Year is timed according to the first full moon in April. Mahayana cultures—in China, Korea, and Vietnam—regard the new year as beginning in January or February, according to the lunar calendar. Japan is the exception: New Year is celebrated on the first day of January.

Other holidays and festivals celebrate the founder of a temple or of a lineage of Buddhism. Mahayana Buddhists celebrate the most significant bodhisattvas, those symbolizing compassion, wisdom, the arts of healing, and more. This means that different Buddhist temples hold festivals on different dates and that from one Buddhist culture to another the schedule of festivals varies considerably.

There is a long-standing tradition of Buddhist travel to the most important sites in the life of the Buddha. Having fallen into disrepair for centuries, these sites are now being revived in a major way, and year-round pilgrimage has become the norm. They include Bodh Gaya, the site of the Buddha's enlightenment experience; Lumbini, where Gautama was born; Sarnath, where the Buddha delivered his first sermon, or sutra; and Kushinagar, where he died and attained parinirvana. These northern Indian areas are no longer primarily inhabited by Buddhists, but the Hindu majority there plays a role in staging these sites for Buddhist pilgrims today.

Although the phrase *Buddhist pilgrimage* still applies in some cases, Buddhist sites have been absorbed into the larger tourist industry, hence the beginnings of widespread Buddhist tourism. With the wealth of many Buddhists today, and the ease of travel that allows anyone to journey to several important Buddhist sites in a single day, Buddhist travelers are visiting the major sites of their tradition in great numbers. In India, in addition to the historic sites just named, there are famous cave grottos and ancient monastic ruins—Sanchi, Ellora, Ajanta, and Nalanda perhaps most famous among them. In Cambodia, Angkor Wat draws millions of tourists, as does the Borobudur stupa in Indonesia. There are numerous ancient pagodas and other Buddhist monuments in Myanmar, located in Mandalay, Pagan, and elsewhere. In Sri Lanka the temple of the Buddha's tooth in Kandy in the central highlands hosts huge numbers of visitors, as do other coastal sites there. In Tibet the Potala Palace has to limit the number of visitors, and in Nepal large crowds gather at several famous pagodas, such as Swayambhunath and Boudhanath. Thailand hosts Buddhist tourists at the ruins of Ayutthaya and at famous temples.

By far the largest group of Buddhist tourists are now Chinese, although there are substantial numbers of Japanese visitors to these sites as well. In China the Buddhist caves at Yungang, Longmen, and Dunhuang are incredible treasures that draw larger and larger groups of Buddhist and other tourists each year. In addition, visitors frequently seek out the four Buddhist sacred mountains, and in the summer, when the cool of the mountains is very attractive, the flow of vacationers to these sacred sites is overwhelming.

A visit to famous temples in Japan and Korea shows the extent of interest in these countries. Welcoming individual pilgrims as well as busloads of schoolchildren, these sites are among the most heavily visited Buddhist locations in the world, especially those in Kyoto, Nara, and Kamakura. Because both Japan and Korea inherited their forms of Buddhism from China, China has now once again become a pilgrimage location for Korean and Japanese visitors. This is especially true of the Zen tradition founded in the beautiful southeastern mountains of China; today more and more visitors make their way to these sacred spots. To mention just one more, on the Japanese island of Shikoku, pilgrims drive, bus, or hike in the steps of the famous master Kukai through eighty-eight temples located along the gorgeous coast. And there are many others. Pilgrimage has been historically and continues to be an important Buddhist practice.

5.19. How have the roles of women in Buddhism changed in contemporary cultures, both in Asia and in the temples and meditation centers of Western Buddhism?

Perhaps the most striking difference between traditional Buddhism and contemporary global Buddhism, especially in the West, is that women are now frequently to be found in leadership positions—as administrative heads of Buddhist institutions, as teachers, and as acclaimed spiritual guides. That Buddhism was being adopted by Western converts at the same historical moment that the feminist movement was taking hold has meant that these two cultural developments would intertwine in a variety of dramatic ways.

The contrast is immediately noticeable. Throughout its long history Buddhism has been dominated by men. This long-standing inclination is a simple function of the fact that Buddhism was generated and sustained in fully patriarchal cultures. Although an order of nuns was instituted by the Buddha himself, ordination has not been available to women in the Theravada countries of Southeast Asia, in Sri Lanka, or in Tibet. A potent cultural tension can be felt almost everywhere in Asia and in Western temples founded by Asian immigrants between preserving valuable traditions and the pull of changing them to align with changing gender norms. The growing empowerment of women has forced the issue of gender parity into Buddhist discussions almost everywhere. Perhaps the most striking example is Thailand, where women are pursuing several channels to make full ordination available to everyone. They argue, as women have elsewhere, that women's distinctive experience provides fresh access to the Buddhist teachings and practices not just for women but for all Buddhists.

In many Western Buddhist centers there are equal numbers of women and men in positions of authority, in both teaching and administration. This is especially noticeable in American Zen but is also increasingly the case at Vipassana meditation centers and elsewhere. In these settings women are active in policy debates, especially those that involve the moral and ethical issues of Buddhist communities. Women are also at the forefront among engaged Buddhists who seek social and environmental justice. One major issue of concern has been the series of revelations about sexual abuse by male teachers in virtually every type of Buddhism. Only very recently have women felt the freedom to discuss this issue openly. Accusations of past transgressions and serious efforts toward policy reforms are now fully under way.

Discussions that began at a conference on women and Buddhism held at Naropa Institute in 1981 have led to a variety of reforms. One of these is the reshaping of Buddhist liturgy so that the traditional patriarchal instincts of earlier traditions are not repeated in current ritual but are instead expressed in gender-neutral language to make it clear that a full range of opportunities is open to women. Another reform has to do with Buddhist lineage charts, which are lists of patriarchs to whom Buddhists are indebted for their inheritance of the Buddhist dharma. These lists are frequently chanted at the beginning of each meditation session. Women participants have noticed the total lack of female representatives, and the reforms under way involve two different tactics. One is research going back through Buddhist archives to locate historic women who in fact made substantial contributions but who were never recognized for their innovative work. The other is to make certain that current women in leadership positions are added to these lists so that their pivotal role in Buddhism is recognized.

Among the Western Buddhist pioneers now well-known for their transformative work within the Buddhist tradition are Jiyu Kennett, Ayya Khema, Maurine Stuart, Ruth Denison, Toni

Packer, Charlotte Joko Beck, Sylvia Boorstein, Pema Chodron, Joan Halifax, Rita Gross, Pat O'Hara, Judith Simmer-Brown, Jan Chozen Bays, and still others. One of the issues that all of these Buddhist women have had to face is the choice between efforts to reform the institutions in which they developed their own Buddhist practice and starting new Buddhist groups that establish gender equality from the very beginning. The original Buddhist insight was that all things are impermanent and open to ongoing change, and Buddhist traditions are clearly feeling that impact today.

5.20. How is the contemporary practice of mindfulness in secular settings such as schools and hospitals related to Buddhist traditions of meditation?

Today the word *mindfulness* is found throughout Western culture and around the world. It refers to a series of mental exercises that train people to be aware of and to focus on whatever experience is occurring in the present moment. To be mindful in this way is to pay precise, nonjudgmental attention to the contents of one's mind. It's that simple, but the positive effects of this exercise are thought to be substantial. Mindfulness is now being taught to children, adolescents, and adults in schools. Hospitals train patients to reduce the negative effects of pain by experiencing it mindfully. Stress-reduction clinics using mindfulness techniques are open in many hospitals. Mindfulness techniques are being used in psychotherapy, in training athletes, in businesses, in prisons, and by people everywhere as a means of enhancing their lives.

To observe the contents of your mind is to avoid distraction and to cease wishing for things to be different than they actually are. That's the meaning of *nonjudgmental* in most definitions of mindfulness. Notice that this means this exercise does not ask participants to stop thinking; instead it asks people simply to be aware that they are thinking and exactly what those thoughts are. It teaches people how to be mindful of what is going on from moment to moment as an exercise of concentration and self-awareness.

Although it is frequently left unsaid, these practices have Buddhist origins. Mindfulness first became a topic of conversation in the English-speaking world with the publication in 1975 of Thich Nhat Hanh's book *The Miracle of Mindfulness: An Introduction to Buddhist Meditation* and with his Buddhist seminars on this topic, which he taught all over the world. But its origins go back to the beginnings of Buddhist teachings on the alleviation of suffering. The Buddha taught people how to stop perpetuating unnecessary suffering caused by trying to avoid all discomfort and pain. Instead he encouraged relaxed, mindful acceptance of discomfort and pain as inevitable dimensions of human life. Many different versions of this basic teaching about suffering have developed throughout the long history of Buddhism.

The early Pali word that is now translated as "mindfulness" is *sati*, also frequently translated as "bare attention." This translation is currently a topic of debate among Buddhist scholars who point out that mindfulness in Pali encompassed more than bare attention because it included being mindful or remembering the teachings of Buddhism concerning suffering and its alleviation. It meant keeping these teachings in mind, which is quite different from simply observing whatever passes through the mind. But however it was named, Buddhist techniques of self-awareness have had a role in mediation practice alongside other practices focused on altering the contents of one's mind. Both have been essential to the highest levels of Buddhist meditation.

The practice of mindfulness began its secular turn in 1979, when Jon Kabat-Zinn founded the Mindfulness-Based Stress Reduction program at the University of Massachusetts. Although a Buddhist practitioner himself, Kabat-Zinn taught chronically ill patients mindfulness without any reference to Buddhism—simply as a medical practice that was successful in reducing stress, pain, and anxiety. Meanwhile, scientific research began to demonstrate that mindfulness practices helped reduce blood pressure, slow heart rate, and ease frenetic brain activity.

The secular functions of mindfulness have branched out in all directions. Clinical psychologists and psychiatrists began to experiment with mindfulness in connection with depression and anxiety and in treatments of drug addiction. Mindfulness instruction was taken into prisons to help men and women calm their anger and begin to reassess their situation in life. Veterans' centers have used mindfulness to help heal the effects of warfare on soldiers' minds. Schools slowly and cautiously experimented with focus and concentration exercises for students; professional athletes began mindfulness training to accompany their rigorous physical training; and even the US Army found ways to put it to use. We are most likely just in the initial stages of the exploration into these kinds of mental training.

The relationship between these secular uses of mindfulness training and uses of it in Buddhist meditation is potentially controversial. Some parents have argued that mindfulness training in schools in the US is unconstitutional based on the separation of church and state. Is this simply "stealth Buddhism" in public schools, as one participant called it? Is the secularization of mindfulness simply a matter of altering vocabulary so that references to Buddhism meditation disappear in favor of the language of contemporary neuroscience? Similar debates have taken place over the various secular uses of yoga, and given the current culture of identity politics there is little chance that these controversies have run their course. If research on the benefits of mindfulness training hold up, however, it is also very likely that we will see more of this practice in the future. Meanwhile, there are Buddhists who complain that secular mindfulness waters down the original so thoroughly that the deepest and most important transformative effects are lost. That argument could very well lead to more Buddhism, not less.

5.21. What are the future prospects for Buddhism?

Buddhist adepts would be smiling broadly at this question, perhaps even laughing uproariously. They might tease us about our motives for asking but would be very unlikely to offer any response that we might consider an answer. History weaves and bends and refuses to conform to prior expectations. And Buddhist teachings relish this stark unknowability of the future. They advise that coming to terms with the openness and unpredictability of life is a major part of wisdom. Although typically foolish enough to attempt predictions anyway, I take this opportunity to bring our questioning to a close—but only temporarily, in hopes that having gotten this far you will take the challenge to push these preliminary explorations and reflections on Buddhism further in your own way.

SUGGESTIONS FOR FURTHER READING

General Introductions and Buddhist History

Carrithers, M. *The Buddha: A Very Short Introduction*. Oxford: Oxford University Press, 2001.

Eckel, Malcolm David. *Buddhism*. Course no. 687. The Great Courses. Audio lectures, 2001.

Fields, Rick. *How the Swans Came to the Lake: A Narrative History of Buddhism in America*. Boston: Shambhala, 1992.

Gethin, Rupert. *The Foundations of Buddhism*. Oxford: Oxford University Press, 1998.

Harvey, Peter. *An Introduction to Buddhism: Teachings, History, Practices*. Cambridge, UK: Cambridge University Press, 2013.

Harvey, Peter. *An Introduction to Buddhist Ethics: Foundations, Values, and Issues*. Cambridge, UK: Cambridge University Press, 2000.

Keown, Damien. *Buddhism: A Very Short Introduction*. Oxford: Oxford University Press, 2013.

Keown, Damien. *Buddhist Ethics: A Very Short Introduction*. Oxford: Oxford University Press, 2005.

Powers, John. *Concise Introduction to Tibetan Buddhism*. Ithaca, NY: Snow Lion, 2008.

Samuel, Geoffrey. *Introducing Tibetan Buddhism*. London: Routledge, 2012.

Skilton, Andrew. *A Concise History of Buddhism*. Birmingham, UK: Windhorse, 1993.

Strong, John. *The Experience of Buddhism: Sources and Interpretations*. Belmont, CA: Wadsworth, 1995.

Williams, Paul. *Buddhist Thought: A Complete Introduction to the Indian Tradition*. London: Routledge, 2011.

Williams, Paul. *Mahayana Buddhism: The Doctrinal Foundations.*
London: Routledge, 1989.

Translations of Buddhist Texts

Bhikku Bodhi. *In the Buddha's Words: An Anthology of Discourses from the
Pali Canon.* Somerville, MA: Wisdom, 2005.

Carter, John Ross, and Mahinda Palihawadana. *The Dhammapada: The
Sayings of the Buddha.* Oxford: Oxford University Press, 1987.

Foster, Nelson, and Jack Shoemaker. *The Roaring Stream: A New Zen
Reader.* Hopewell, NJ: Ecco Press, 1996.

Gethin, Rupert. *Sayings of the Buddha: New Translations from the Pali
Nikayas.* Oxford: Oxford University Press, 2008.

Shantideva. *The Bodhicaryavatara.* Translated by Kate Crosby and
Andrew Skilton. Oxford: Oxford University Press, 1996.

Tanahashi, Kazuaki, and Peter Levitt. *The Essential Dogen.*
Boston: Shambhala, 2013.

Thanissaro Bhikku. *The Wings to Awakening: An Anthology from the Pali
Canon.* Barre, MA: Dhamma Dana, 1996.

Thich Nhat Hanh. *The Diamond That Cuts through Illusion.* Berkeley,
CA: Paralax Press, 1992.

Thurman, Robert. *The Holy Teaching of Vimalakirti: A Mahayana Scripture.*
University Park, PA: Penn State University Press, 1976.

Teachings and Practices

Chogyam Trungpa. *The Bodhisattva Path of Wisdom and Compassion.*
Boston: Shambhala, 2014.

Chogyam Trungpa. *Cutting through Spiritual Materialism.*
Boston: Shambhala, 1973.

Dalai Lama. *The Art of Happiness.* New York: Riverhead Books, 2009.

Kasulis, T. P. *Zen Action: Zen Person.* Honolulu: University of Hawaii
Press, 1990.

Lopez, Donald. *Buddhism in Practice.* Princeton, NJ: Princeton
University Press, 1995.

Pema Chodron. *Comfortable with Uncertainty: 108 Teachings.*
Boston: Shambhala, 2002.

Suzuki, Shunryu. *Zen Mind, Beginner's Mind.*
New York: Weatherhill, 1970.

Thich Nhat Hanh. *Essential Writings.* New York: Orbis Books, 2001.

Wright, Dale. *The Six Perfections: Buddhism and the Cultivation of
Character.* Oxford: Oxford University Press, 2009.

Meditation

Brach, Tara. *Radical Acceptance: Embracing Your Life with the Heart of a Buddha*. New York: Bantam, 2004.

Brahm, Ajahn. *Mindfulness, Bliss, and Beyond: A Meditator's Handbook*. Somerville, MA: Wisdom, 2006.

Goldstein, Joseph. *Insight Meditation: The Practice of Freedom*. Boston: Shambhala, 2003.

Goldstein, Joseph. *Mindfulness: A Practical Guide to Awakening*. Boulder, CO: Sounds True, 2013.

Goleman, Daniel. *The Meditative Mind: The Varieties of Meditative Experience*. New York: Putnam, 1988.

Kabat-Zinn, Jon. *Mindfulness for Beginners*. Boulder, CO: Sounds True, 2012.

Kornfield, Jack. *Meditation for Beginners*. Louisville, KY: Sounds True, 2008.

Nyanoponkia Thera. *The Heart of Buddhist Meditation*. New York: Samuel Weiser, 1962.

Pema Chodron. *How to Meditate*. Boulder, CO: Sounds True, 2013.

Rosenberg, Larry. *Breath by Breath: The Liberating Practice of Insight Meditation*. Boston: Shambhala, 2004.

Thich Nhat Hanh. *The Miracle of Mindfulness*. Boston: Beacon Press, 1976.

Contemporary Buddhism

Batchelor, Stephen. *After Buddhism: Rethinking the Dharma for a Secular Age*. New Haven, CT: Yale University Press, 2015.

Batchelor, Stephen. *The Awakening of the West: The Encounter of Buddhism and Western Culture*. Berkeley, CA: Paralax, 1994.

Buswell, Robert. *The Zen Monastic Experience: Buddhist Practice in Contemporary Korea*. Princeton, NJ: Princeton University Press, 1992.

Dalai Lama. *My Spiritual Journey*. New York: HarperOne, 2010.

Goldstein, Joseph. *One Dharma: The Emerging Western Buddhism*. New York: HarperCollins, 2002.

Hanson, Rick, and Richard Mendius. *The Buddha's Brain*. Oakland, CA: New Harbinger Press, 2009.

Kaza, Stephanie. *Mindfully Green*. Boston: Shambhala, 2008.

Kaza, Stephanie, and Kenneth Kraft. *Dharma Rain: Sources of Buddhist Environmentalism*. Boston: Shambhala, 1999.

Loy, David. *The Great Awakening: A Buddhist Social Theory*. Boston: Wisdom, 2003.

Queen, Christopher. *Engaged Buddhism in the West*. Somerville, MA: Wisdom, 2000.

Queen, Christopher, and Sallie King, eds. *Engaged Buddhism: Buddhist Liberation Movements in Asia*. Albany, NY: SUNY Press, 1996.

Wright, Robert. *Why Buddhism Is True: The Science and Philosophy of Meditation and Enlightenment*. New York: Simon and Schuster, 2017.

INDEX

For the benefit of digital users, indexed terms that span two pages (e.g., 52–53) may, on occasion, appear on only one of those pages.

Abhidharma, 20–21, 26
Afghanistan, 36, 38, 47
Alara Kalama, 9–10
Ambedkar, B.R., 66–67, 194–95
Amitabha Buddha (Amida), 104–5, 108–9, 133–34, 154
Anagarika Dharmapala, 195–96
Ananda, 16, 26–27, 32
anatman (no self), 77, 81, 83, 114
Angkor Wat, 207–8
arhat, 32–33, 140
Arnold, Sir Edwin, 66
art, 152
asceticism, 10, 14–15, 142
Ashoka, 33–34, 35, 39, 171–72
Avalokitesvara, 184
Avatamsaka sutra, 141

Baizhang, 161–62
Bangladesh, 35, 190
Batchelor, Stephen, 183–84
begging, 23, 145
Benares (Varanasi), 6, 11, 151
bhavana, 125–26
Bodh Gaya, 6, 149, 151, 195–96, 207

bodhi tree, 10–11, 149–50, 151, 163
bodhicitta (thought of enlightenment), 95, 139, 157
Bodhidharma, 60–61, 109–10
bodhisattva, 97, 98, 100, 115–16, 141, 200–1
Bon, 54–55
Borobudur, 207–8
Buddha nature, 60, 106–7, 111, 158
Buddhacarita, 11–12, 45–46
Buddhaghosa, 45–46
Buddhism as religion, 29, 31, 165
Buddhist councils, 32, 37, 38
Buddhist modernism, 64–65, 66, 173, 187–88

Cambodia, 35, 37–38, 39
capitalism, 175, 192–93
caste system, 25, 66–67, 159, 194–95
chanting, 95–96, 108, 131–32, 149, 153–54, 162
Cheng Yen, 199
China, 36, 38, 47, 48, 51, 55, 59–60, 196
Chogyam Trungpa, 69–70, 188–89

Christianity, 6, 27, 46, 64–65, 96,
    108–9, 170
Confucianism, 49–51, 53
cosmology, 93
cultural revolution, 197
Cunda, 31

Dalai Lama, 57, 69–70, 164, 174,
    184, 190–91, 195, 201
Daoism, 50–51, 53, 62
dependent arising, 77, 79, 81, 114
Dhammapada, 45
dharma, 28, 32, 71, 72, 167–68
dhyana, 59–60
Diamond sutra, 44
Dogen, 111
dukkha (suffering), 71, 72, 75,
    76, 78
Dunhuang, 47–48, 208

ecoBuddhism, 191
eightfold path, 74, 123–24
emptiness (sunyata), 97–98, 100,
    105–6, 156–57
encounter dialogue, 61
Engaged Buddhism, 66–67,
    141–42, 172–73
enlightenment (awakening), 10,
    74, 97, 100, 103–4,
    106–7, 116, 122–23
eternalism, 80, 82, 117–18

faith, 95, 109, 136, 167
festivals, 206
five ascetics, 10–11
five hindrances, 116, 126
five skandhas (aggregates),
    83, 117–18
Fo Guang Shan, 198–99, 200
four immeasurables, 114–15, 117
four noble truths, 72, 79

Genghis Khan, 57
Geshe Wangyal, 69–70

Goenka, S.N., 187–88
Goldstein, Joseph, 69, 187–88
Goleman, Daniel, 187–88

Healing Buddha, 104–5
Heart sutra, 162
Hinayana, 37–38, 41–42, 96–97
Hinduism, 28, 39, 63, 66–67, 88,
    105, 170, 194–95
Hsing Yun, 200
Huayan, 53–54

impermanence, 31, 77, 78, 114
Indonesia, 35
Indus valley, 7, 36
Islam, 6, 27, 36, 47, 64, 170

Japan, 36, 38, 51, 59–60
Jataka Tales, 45–46
Jokhang Temple, 202–3

Kabat-Zinn, Jon, 212–13
Kalama sutra, 72, 96
Kamalasila, 55
Kanjur, 52
Kapilavastu, 8
karma, 25–26, 86, 88, 91, 121
Kaundinya, 16
kensho, 60–61
Kerouac, Jack, 70
Korea, 36, 38, 51, 59–60
Kornfield, Jack, 69, 187–88
Kusana Empire, 47
Kushinagar, 30, 151, 207

Lalitavistara, 11–12
Lama, 52, 58–59, 69–70, 155
Laos, 37–38, 39
Linji, 46
Lotus sutra, 96, 107–8, 155
Lumbini, 8, 149, 150–51, 207

Madhyamaka, 105
Maha Bodhi Society, 195–96

Mahakasyapa, 60–61, 112–13
Mahasiddhas, 58
Mahavastu, 11–12, 45–46
Mahayana, 36, 42, 43, 49, 96, 98,
    100, 102, 136–37, 163
Maitreya, 104–5
Malaysia, 35
mandala, 146–47, 158
mantra, 146–47, 158
Mao Zedong, 196–97
Mara, 10–11
meditation, 24–25, 60, 86, 115–16,
    123, 125, 126, 130, 134, 137,
    160–61, 178, 211
merit, 24
middle path, 14, 21, 80, 82,
    117–18, 142
Milarepa, 143
Milindapanha, 45–46, 81–82
mind to mind transmission,
    60–61, 112–13
mindfulness, 60, 127–28, 131, 132,
    178, 211
Mogao caves, 47–48
morality (*sila*), 21, 24, 25, 91, 113,
    123, 137
Mount Hiei, 144
Mount Kailash, 144
mudras, 146–47, 150, 158
Mulamadhyamika karikas, 45–46
Myanmar, 35, 37–38, 39,
    187–88, 190–91

Naropa University, 69–70, 173–74,
    188–89, 210
Navayana, 66–67
nembutsu, 108–9, 133–34, 154
Neo-Confucian, 50–51
nihilism, 80, 82, 101–2, 117–18
nirvana, 31–32, 72–73, 82, 87, 100,
    116, 140
non-dualism, 100, 101–2,
    105–6, 110–11
non-injury (*ahimsa*), 189, 192

ordination, 21–22, 146, 209

Pakistan, 36, 38
Pali, 27, 32–33, 38, 42
Pali canon, 26, 43
parinirvana, 31–32, 102–3, 117–18
Peace Fellowship, 191
Pema Chodron, 46
Perfection of wisdom sutras, 41–42,
    100–1, 154
pilgrimage, 150, 206
Potala Palace, 202–3, 207–8
prayer, 136
precepts, 113–14, 138
psychology, 169, 178
Pure Land Buddhism, 53–54, 108–
    9, 133–34, 137
Pure Land sutras, 96, 108–9

Qing Dynasty, 57

Rajagraha, 32
rebirth, 88, 91
Rohingya Muslims, 190–91

Salzberg, Sharon, 69, 187–88.
samadhi, 127
samsara, 92, 97, 100
San Francisco Zen Center, 70, 188
sangha, 17, 20, 23, 25, 31, 32, 39–40,
    154, 171
Sanskrit, 42, 59–60
satori, 60–61
science, 64–65, 169, 173
scripture, 26, 40, 42, 147
secular Buddhism 181
seed of Buddhahood, 59, 62, 98,
    99, 106–7, 156–57
sesshin, 160–61
Shakyamuni, 13
shamatha, 126, 157
Shantideva, 46, 133
Shariputra, 16
Shinran, 46, 108–9

Siddhartha, 8, 12–13
siddhis, 58
Silk Road, 36, 38, 46, 48–49, 54
Singapore, 35
six perfections, 99–100, 115–16
skillful means (*upaya*), 98, 106
Snyder, Gary, 70, 193–94
Soto zen, 111, 188
Soyen Shaku, 66
Sri Lanka, 35, 37–38, 39, 143
stream winner, 140
stupa, 31, 149
sutras (suttas), 11–12, 26, 28, 36,
    42, 43, 50, 56, 97, 107–8, 141
Suzuki, D.T., 66, 70
Suzuki, Shunryu, 70, 188

taisho tripitaka, 52
Tang dynasty, 50, 53–54
tanha (thirst, craving), 73–74
Tantras, 58–59
Tantric, 56–57, 58, 105, 146–47,
    154, 156
Tarthang Tulku, 69–70
Tathagata, 14
ten fetters, 140
Tenjur, 52
Thailand, 35, 37–38, 39, 155
Theravada, 36, 39, 79–80, 96–97,
    118, 136, 152
Therigata, 19–20
Thich Nhat Hanh, 46, 172–73,
    186–87, 190–91, 193–94, 212
three jewels (refuges), 95–96,
    102–3, 107, 131–32, 136, 157
three poisons, 76, 87–88,
    120–21, 189–90

Tibet, 36, 38, 54, 58, 69–70, 155,
    156, 184, 195, 201
Tientai (Tendai), 53–54
transmission of the lamp, 61
trikaya (three bodies), 103
tripitaka, 26, 38
Tsongkhapa, 46

Uddaka Ramaputta, 10
Upanisads, 8

Vairocana Buddha, 104–5
Vajrayana, 38–39, 58, 105, 156
Vasubhandu, 46
Vedic culture, 7, 25
Vesak, 206–7
Vietnam, 35, 36, 38, 51,
    63, 172–73
Vimalakirti sutra, 102, 105–6,
    110–11, 176
vinaya, 10–11, 20, 26, 32, 37,
    45–46, 98
vipassana, 69, 126, 157, 187–88
Visuddhimagga, 45–46
vow of compassion, 97, 98–99,
    163, 200–1

Western Buddhism, 67, 181
Wings to Awakening 30–31
World Parliament of
    Religions, 66

Yogacara, 105

zazen, 60
Zen (Chan, Son), 59, 66, 69–70,
    109, 119, 148–49, 152–53, 159